LATE JOURNALS

Also by Antigone Kefala

The Alien
The First Journey
Thirsty Weather
The Island
Alexia: A Tale of Two Cultures
European Notebook
Absence: New and Selected Poems
Summer Visit: Three Novellas
Sydney Journals
Max: The Confessions of a Cat
Fragments

ANTIGONE KEFALA

LATE JOURNALS

REFLECTIONS 2000–2020

Published 2022
from the Writing and Society Research Centre
at Western Sydney University
by the Giramondo Publishing Company
PO Box 752
Artarmon NSW 1570 Australia
www.giramondopublishing.com

Designed by Jenny Grigg
Typeset by Andrew Davies
in Tiempos Regular 9/15pt

Printed and bound by Ligare Book Printers
Distributed in Australia by NewSouth Books

A catalogue record for this book is available from the National Library of Australia.

ISBN 978-1-925818-97-0

9 8 7 6 5 4 3 2 1

The Giramondo Publishing Company acknowledges the support of Western Sydney University in the implementation of its book publishing program.

This project has been assisted by the Commonwealth Government through the Australia Council, its arts funding and advisory body.

Contents

Journal I

January

Last night at the Opera House to see the Argentinian tango. We booked too late and could only find tickets in the front row. We could not see the dancers' feet when too close to us, nor half of the bodies of the musicians.

A clean, muscular performance, interesting dissonant music, the woman dancer very beautiful. More like acrobats.

A lot of showmanship, but little passion or inner movement. A perfect outside imitation of a tango passion they could not bring to life.

The second male dancer a very interesting face, as if Russian, the three of them impeccably dressed.

A stylised machismo, but the woman responding with equal force, so that you had a balanced distribution of energies.

Re-reading *Interviews with Film Directors* edited by Andrew Sarris.

In his introduction he is discussing film techniques, directorial styles and so on...

The choice between a close-up and a long shot, for example, may quite transcend the plot.

If the story of Little Red Riding Hood is told with the Wolf in close-up and the Little Red Riding Hood in long shot, the director is concerned primarily with the emotional problems of the Wolf with a compulsion to eat little girls.

If Little Red Riding Hood is in close-up and the Wolf in long shot, the emphasis has shifted to the emotional problems of vestigial virginity in a wicked world...

Thus two different stories are being told with the same basic anecdotal material...

What is at stake in the two versions of Little Red Riding Hood are two contrasting directorial attitudes towards life...

Sarris's book is dedicated to his mother Themis and his brother George, and all the little film magazines that have kept the faith despite inadequate funding.

We went to see the exhibition in the old house and gallery. We had not been there for a long time, when we used to come for picnics on the old verandah with the kids, in summer. Ileana, very small and philosophical-looking, full of interest for things around her, textures, the movement of trees which she was trying to imitate with her small hands, her blue eyes marvellously deep, a real person already.

We stayed there on the verandah talking, eating, laughing. Very few people on the grounds, the day very hot, and then a short, heavy rain, the scent of the earth and the heat rising from the ground and behind us the galleries, closed in their air-conditioned perfection.

The landscape outside bleached in the heat, the grass brown, the small hills looking like an early Nolan – *Wimmera*.

February

We went to hear Hilik speaking at the SQUAT. The young were cooking, some came with cooked food. All these squatters, young, vulnerable looking, some amazing hairdos, partly shaved heads, rings through their lips, tattoos...

Squatting upstairs and in some empty houses nearby.

Some of them artists, radio people, some wanting to be writers. A friendly atmosphere of broken-down chairs, cedar staircase painted black, all trying to escape into a freer world.

During Hilik's talk, about sculpture, his sculptures, at one point, near the kitchen some talk, the level rather high, and the young man who introduced Hilik calling out:

'Silence please. An artist is speaking.'

I rather liked that.

Reading the new book. The poems, as if constantly saying something, yet an empty sort of phenomenon, like an artificial essence they put into drinks to make people want to drink more, but which leaves them empty.

Afternoon, white light.

Hot dry wind blowing on the terrace. Tight, stretched blue sky.

A summer afternoon as in Brăila, only I left to remember it.

Reading again *Sviatoslav Richter: Notebooks and Conversations*, with an introduction by Bruno Monsaingeon, who made a documentary about him...

As an antidote to anxiety, he is listening to records, his own and others, painting, looking at films...he appeared in a film about Glinka playing Liszt.

Watching a film by Tony Palmer about Maria Callas, a film he does not like...'made by people with no talent who are unworthy of their subject.'

He writes: 'Maria's last words as Jacques, Christian and I were setting off downstairs after the only visit that I paid her in her flat in Paris were:

"Don't forget me and never break the thread that binds us together."'

– Amen –

At Beth and Warwick's last night.

We looked at Beth's latest work using Australian grasses. Very detailed, fine work, this amazing shoe made of grasses that looks like a Magritte apparition.

The rest too, implements, guns, an abstracted version of implements used by the colonists to tame the land.

The exhibition in Canberra.

March

They were discussing memories of childhood.

Thinking of mine:

Instruments, music, struggles with music, instruments that had to be played again and again to yield music.

BOOKS, books, books, reading them, discussing them, life evoked in books.

Lectures, concerts, theatre, films, walks, summer, winter, autumn, acacias, the Danube, the gardens, statues, revolutions, war, problems, the moon, fear, bombs, material unease, illness, desperation.

Reading some tankas by Takuboku Ishikawa (1886–1912):

When I breathe
This sound in my chest
Lonelier than a winter wind…

It made me think of Mother.

Fellini:

'The visionary is the only true realist.'

In the magazine writers describing their difficulties with writing.

He was describing his efforts to become part of the Australian scene after he migrated here with his parents, by trying to mirror Aboriginal writing and approaches, to be told off by an Aboriginal writer with whom he shared a platform at a reading.

I thought last night – a deeper alienation than mine.

In my case neither mirroring nor mimesis, from when we left Romania, and even before that, I was aware that I was trespassing on someone else's territory. Constantly trying not to venture on their patch, appropriate, trying to define my limits, my territory, mostly inwardly, my experience, finding a language for it.

In spite of the intellectual gloss of the paper, nothing but inner desperation.

Late on SBS a program on the SUN. What mysteries! What forces! And its eventual, possible annihilation and we with it.

A dark hypothesis, or more factual knowledge?

Who knows finally the essence of the universe?

I went to bed. I could not sleep for a long time.

Unsettling forces at work.

The programme finished with the American Indians doing a dance to thank the Sun for looking after us.

Who knows to what forces the planet responds...

A description of Australia as:

'The most flammable continent.'

Agnes Varda and her film *The Gleaners* –

After it was shown people wrote to her about what they were gathering too.

This young woman gathering small objects that people were throwing away, she called the pieces:

Des Objets Inconsolable

Inconsolable objects.

Discussions about the Nobel Prize and who got it.

When Beckett got it, the response of his wife Suzanne: 'Quelle catastrophe!'

An article about Georges Perros, the French writer.

He has a sensitive spot for the hard work and isolation of writing, the estrangement from self and family and the impossibility of simultaneous connection to one's readers: 'Writing is saying something to someone who is not there. Who will never be there. Or if he is there, we'll be the ones who have gone away.'

Ivor rings in the afternoon:

'Has the ABC started to broadcast *Summer Visit*?'

He was in Berkelouw's, a man ran in and demanded a copy of the book.

I was laughing:

'You should have photographed him immediately.'

FINALLY A READER!

Archbishop Stylianos very enthusiastic about his poetry book and the translations.

He is always vital, full of energy, grasping the language full on, as in his poetry.

He is pleased when something is good, we are all part of things, sitting together at the same table.

The translations work well, his only uncertainty – the numinous – he feels should have been *to theion*.

I said: 'Send us your alternatives.'

'No, no,' he said, 'just an impression, the things are good as they stand, we must not undermine their value with small stuff.'

He was complaining that there is so little response.

He thinks that the community should stir itself and become an active part of the scene.

April

A peaceful night, we came on the terrace, a light wind was blowing, the moon was rising on the right of the bridge, the little train was rattling in the wind.

At the dinner, Julie, who does not seem to like me...I was making some ironic remark that with the Bicentennial money, every small town has now a bronze statue of a shearer. And she, in an acrid tone: 'Why shouldn't they have it?'

I did not reply, but plenty of other things to be celebrated, the statue of a woman pioneer, a country singer, a poet...Why would a shearer be considered the essence of Australia?

A dove crying in the tree and the garden full of pigeons resting on the grass, fanning their wings in the sun, sparrows finding tidbits...

Bruce rang from Hamburg. A long conversation which always starts with the state of his health – not good.

His wife is translating his poems into German, they sound quite pompous, as if Goebbels had written them.

Each language carries its own past.

Australia, he feels, a place of sun, space, people responding more directly to life.

At the end of some television programme – there is the Opera House, Bondi Beach and a sunset.

'Propaganda! Propaganda!' I said laughing, he was laughing too.

Vivienne describing the attitude of the young to us: 'They think we are camphorised.'

Angelopoulos's small film in black-and-white in memory of Mastroianni, with Jeanne Moreau.

In an interesting building, elegant staircase, umbrellas, rain, and Moreau with a ravaged face, beautiful but sad, with a strong voice.

Moreau: 'My face has changed with the years and has enough history in it to give audiences something to work with.'

In *The Guardian*, a review by Peter Conrad of a new biography of Proust by William C. Carter.

'Despite his neurasthenia, the ferocity of his ambition was positively Napoleonic.'

May

On Sunday, when I woke up the rain was sifting down.

I and a pigeon in the tree watching the rain over the city, the sun, suddenly out, a transparent, luminous curtain behind the fog.

The pepper tree – shredded silk moving in a green wind.

Reading Plath, *Ariel*, very good, a destructive sort of energy in the poems, but amazingly well caught. Dark chasm, terrors all around, a constant and painful exposure with nothing to protect one.

'The Rival', 'The Arrival of the Bee Box', 'Edge' – a dead woman with her two dead children by her side, perfect in death.

Plath – a tortured woman, a sort of Celan but in a more shrilled tone and more self-obsessed.

An interview with Don Hany in *The Australian* by Megan

Lehman. Hany comes out as an intelligent, thinking person, more complex answers to the questions than it is usual in such interviews. Quoting from the interview:

'A lot of *East West 101* was an attempt to make a show about multiculturalism,' he says.

'Really, it was just an exercise in colour-blind casting. Australian popular culture resolutely ignores the reality of a multicultural society.

'It is amazing how our television can depict just one part of our culture and how generally satisfying that can be for Australian audience's appetites.

'What we need to do is cast Australians you see walking down Pitt Street and create stories around the diversity of our people, as opposed to making shows about multiculturalism or about racial tensions in our cities. What all these shows end up doing is making a gap between mainstream audiences and our minority audience.'

Looking at a documentary on Rubinstein.

'It is simply my life, music, I live it, breathe it, talk with it.'

He lost his entire family in the Holocaust. He never played in Germany.

Interviews in French, Italian, Spanish, English.

In the Spanish interview he was being asked whether he believed in life after death. His response:

'Frankly, no.'

But if there is, he would be delighted, more than delighted.

June

A programme on the COMPUTER – new communications, cheaper rates, contact with the world, more information about the world, making friends with the world.

But I feel that there is already a lot of misplaced information everywhere.

We don't know what to do with it, how to integrate it in our lives, and what it means ultimately to know all this undigested, unplaced information.

A new method of running away from oneself, listening less and less to oneself, everything finally simulated.

An exhibition of the American artist James Castle. One of the gallery directors analysing his work:

'What is an artist but a person who wills a form into being that did not exist before.'

What a relief to have got over the Poetry Reading. A very friendly audience.

Ileana describing the reading as – FANTASTIC – I said laughing:

'This is the type of reaction we want to hear.'

In an essay by Philip Roth written some forty years earlier:

'Actuality is constantly outdoing our talents, and the culture tosses up figures, almost daily, that are the envy of a novelist.'

Two kookaburras waiting silently on the fence, a very unusual sight, looking carefully at the neighbour's garden.

No sound out of them. Short and stocky somehow, and cuddly in spite of their ferocious voice, that seemed sinister the first time I heard them.

Their pointed beaks in a dark mauve colour.

Writers and critics. An arid period for writers, at least for writers like myself.

All criticism focused on THEORY, squeezing the texts to prove the theories, an arid inversion somehow.

Jolanta walking by the sea this morning, her last walk before travelling overseas.

The surface of the sea as if full of diamonds, the sun was rising, breaking on the waters...

'Very beautiful...very beautiful...' she kept saying.

'I can't remember what I was before I met you, just emptiness when I think of it – I was not living.'

Gregory Peck confessing to a beautiful woman, in a black-and-white film, on late-night television.

July

Isaac Babel:

'No iron can pierce the heart with such force as a full stop at the right place.'

Kandinsky:

'The more frightening the world becomes, the more art becomes abstract.'

Reading Pliny the Younger writing to Emperor Trajan. The tone of the letters of a lawyer, but not legalese. He was dealing with an assortment of problems as governor of Bithynia – public structures, canals to the sea, fire precautions, religious observances, trials, disputes and so on. The tone of the letters, Trajan's answers, as if between a higher and a lower order, but not fulsome or condescending.

Public buildings, the fire that destroyed the Elder Citizens' Club. So they had them too, probably this is where they originated.

Gymnasiums – Trajan in a letter:

'These poor Greeks, they all love a gymnasium.'

In the meantime, while they were deifying the emperors and offering them sacrifices, they found the Christians fanatics. Pliny tells Trajan how he is dealing with the Christians, asking them to renounce their faith etc. etc.…if not they are punished, executed.

Pliny tells him that an anonymous pamphlet was circulated with their names. Trajan's response:

'But pamphlets, circulating anonymously, must play no part in any accusation. They create the worst kind of precedent and are quite out of keeping with the spirit of our age.'

Raining constantly and cold. The crows calling out from the trees like people suffering.

In the corner shop, this elderly man with an interesting head but looking quite neglected.

Did I have a sister that lived in Trafalgar Street? I said no.

He – 'I look very much like her, but she has passed away.' An echo of things to come.

Thinking of Mother, discussions over the years, this maze of feelings that I was constantly talking about, feelings as yet unformed, intellectualities that were borrowed, propensities towards some nebulous possibilities of life, this reaching out towards something ungrasped, ungraspable...She was always listening to all this, with understanding, offering advice from time to time, afraid to a certain extent of what might come.

The resonance of things in me so powerful that any small sound in myself, became like a wind...a feeling of constant exposure...

Emily Dickinson:

'To live is so startling it leaves time for little else.'

She is right, as always.

Writing – a sort of resurrection of life...lived...

We are constantly trying to create the illusion of life, of permanence...

August

I was complaining that she had not written a letter for a long time. But she was excited, she had gone on FACEBOOK, wrote impressions of her travels, performances she had seen…amazing how people responded.

We are being forgotten in favour of FACEBOOK, TWITTER… Everyone is going public. Conversations with the world! While the intimate exchange is ignored.

Reading magazines, like a poison that leaves you empty. Voices that seem to rise to tell you of exciting things, but when you look closer, everything full of a false gloss. Colour, photographs, advertisements, books always described as amazing, experimental…

The advertisements more and more dramatic.

An enormous discrepancy between the values of actual life and the noisy presentation of them.

Warwick and Beth talking of St Petersburg, which they had just visited. The buildings totally reconstructed after the war, with enormous craftmanship.

Very hot while they were there. The Russians complaining of the heat…it has never been that hot…

But Warwick was reading *Crime and Punishment*, a summer like this in the eighteen hundreds…

Erik Satie:

'We don't savour the state of poverty enough, and this is a sign of very serious disorder.'

Ion Mureşan – Romanian poet – in The Poetry International Archives.

'Asked whether too much poetry is being written today, Ion Mureşan replied that there can never be too many poets and that they are all important, no matter whether they write well or badly. Just as our bodies produce antibodies to fight an infection, a sick society produces poets. "The poets are white blood cells, antibodies that fight off a bad idea, corruption or a vulgar use of language."

'And just as every antibody is important in surrounding and making a germ harmless, every poet is important, even if he only reads his work in his own flat in the presence of a small group of friends.'

'Although his work has a confessional character, Ion Mureşan adds that his own life doesn't make much of an appearance in his poems and then only fragmentarily – "I always try and write in the name of my neighbours."'

Fidelio last night.

Dear Beethoven – love, justice and peace.

The music very moving, the production well put together.

The opening of the second act, Julian Gavin singing Florestan. Beautiful sounds that seem adequate in terms of the prisoner's experience – the lyricism of desperation very well conveyed.

Abbado conducting Mozart's Requiem in Salzburg with the Berlin Philharmonic, in memory of Karajan.

Conducting without a score, gathering them all – the large Swedish choir, the soloists, the orchestra, gathering them with slow soft movements, singing the words at every entry.

The well-known writer being interviewed, his early readings of literature...*Wuthering Heights, Bleak House, The Hunchback of Notre Dame*...

What he discovered in these novels was sex fetishised and sublimated but all the more titillating for that.

Dickens, he says, was a master of fetishised sex, once your eyes are open to it. Reading Dickens is like reading Dr Hirschfeld's *Sexual Anomalies and Perversions*...Obviously, what everyone brings to literature is themselves.

Reading a biography of Bergman, his films, a part of our lives. He seemed to have had the same need for emotional warmth that we all have.

Then going to town on Friday, the bus full. A couple came in with a little girl. She very Scandinavian looking, blonde, high cheek bones, he dark, with very dark eyes and a little beard, a cap, looking very much like Bergman in the photos.

Suddenly one realises the difference between a photo and the living person, this vitality in the air emanating from the person, an explosiveness of silent energy that can only be hinted at in a photo.

He looked amazingly like Bergman – a superimposition by me? He was at ease, talking to the little girl.

One understood suddenly the impact the living Bergman would have had on those around him.

Philip Guston, the American painter:

'When you start working everybody is in your studio – the past, your friends, your enemies, the art world and above all, your own ideas – are all there.

But as you continue painting, they start leaving one by one, and you are left completely alone.

Then, if you are lucky, even you leave.'

A quote from Max Beerbohm that we can well apply to the current scene:

'A man whose career was glorious without intermission, decade after decade, does surely try our patience.' From his essay 'Quia Imperfectum'.

Saturday night, strong wind, the tree moving from side to side, brushing the face of the moon, round and luminous.

A party going on in the neighbourhood.

Thinking of Eve, her death, such a closure, nothing matters now. The importance and weight of all her gestures totally demolished.

September

Fay Zwicky on the ABC, speaking enthusiastically about Chaucer...but describing Eliot as a 'dyspeptic writer'.

Dyspeptic reminds me of Molière and *Le Malade Imaginaire*.

Showing Leslie the cockatoo that has been coming here for a few weeks, with rather dirty, tattered feathers, breaking off soft parts of the branches and throwing them down, moving its heavy weight on branches that can't sustain its weight, as if not used to the environment.

Leslie thinks that he is an elderly cocky that was probably in a cage for a long time.

Then she gave me this amazing fact that they can live in sheltered condition to one hundred years.

I said: 'Are we looking at a nineteenth-century cocky?'

Reading a small biography of Cossington-Smith. The phenomenon of someone of such calibre working for so long unrecognised, till she was almost eighty. An old story.

While everyone now thinks that they can pick up a genius at first glance. As Pat used to tell me, that if my painter friends are not making it, it is because they are no good, because now, everyone is on the lookout for talent.

But the question remains, they may be on the lookout, but WHAT ARE THEY CAPABLE OF SEEING?

In the gallery her paintings seemed at rest, a calming effect, her Harbour Bridge massive, the weight palpable in spite of the lightness of the colours.

Len Evans has died too. They were having a wake in a vineyard, discussing his life, his beginnings.

The restaurant he opened, early on, in the old Sydney Stock Exchange, where you could eat and get a glass of wine, where we used to go after work with Joan, and feel very daring and adventurous.

On Sunday we watched Nadine's film on David Boyd.

His paintings more interesting than Arthur's, yet he was not given Arthur's celebrity status.

The only book I have on him and Hermia, is the pottery book. His paintings – early series of explorers, before Tucker, I think, the Aboriginal disasters and so on…

A lively, warm personality, travelling and living in Europe, fond of his family.

In a series of Australian animals he referred to the WOMBAT as EVERYMAN. I should tell Yolanta, she made some sculptures of wombats and is very fond of them.

De Chirico:

'There are more enigmas in the shadow of a man who walks in the sun, than in all the religions of the past, the present and the future.'

In Canberra with JJ. Beautiful weather.

Canberra full of wattle trees in flower, the pink and white Japanese trees. The exhibitions very good.

Frida Kahlo, a concentrated intensity, amazing details, especially in *The Bride*, very beautiful work.

Hester – fluid, quirky, a dramatic line that nevertheless has an amazing calming effect, like good works of art.

We were all enthusiastic. My favourite – *Young Girl With A Dog*, well resolved, visually warm.

Spring, fragile weather, the trees in bloom, the birds running about with their spring duties, the scent of jasmine from the garden next door, but the humans, a terrible race.

Everywhere nothing but negative news, killings, more and more disasters, the press totally feeding this type of approach. We have been transformed into voyeurists…more crying…more deaths, everyone praying, lighting candles, bringing flowers... But this praying does not seem to change anyone, we go on killing each other.

The holy book in one hand and the gun in the other – the old approach.

October

Last night at the opening and then dinner. Jurgis all over the place, stories about Murmansk, my black shoes that look like the ones worn by Lucrezia Borgia in the painting...Unnerved by the death of Horace, the neighbour that used to visit him, who died within three months of prostate cancer.

Horace – brought up by his aunts, his mother did not want to have anything to do with him. Did not remember his father. Did not know who he was. A rape?

His aunts very strict, he was not allowed to go out into the world for fear that the world will damage him.

Never travelled anywhere further than Granville, in Sydney. He used to drop by and have cups of tea with Jurgis.

Jurgis went to his funeral yesterday.

Quotes from Max Frisch:

'Technology is a way of organising the universe so that man does not have to experience it.'

The last instalment on TV of the *Bush Mechanics*.

Very lovely, the countryside, their ingenuity, paintings as a currency to be exchanged. Speaking their language like the sound of a creek flowing, the sound of running water.

And the landscape, last night travelling to Broome, out of their country, 'we are strangers here,' they said.

For every natural phenomenon that we attribute to physical forces they said: 'Who is bringing this on us? Maybe because we killed the snake.' The whole thing very human.

Mary saying how stubborn nature is, on and on, all these dreadful plants that have roots that stretch for two miles, she is trying to get rid of them.

How Nature should take a rest.

I said, everything wants to live, and as regards Nature, I thought, fear, fear of being annihilated.

A review of a new translation of a book by Voltaire, *A Pocket Philosophical Dictionary*, published by Oxford University Press, translated by John Fletcher.

The reviewer – David Coward:

'The seventy-three short essays of Voltaire's *Dictionnaire Philosophique Portatif* (1764), provide an alphabetical account of everything he thought about this world and the next.

'Voltaire's wry, sharp, alphabetical demolition of fuzzy thinking and obscurantism signposts the Enlightenment way to progress.

'"All it takes," he wrote to a correspondent, is: "to bow to God, practise virtue and believe that two and two make four."'

November

An article in the *New Yorker* about Barzun who is 100. He was being quoted:

'Old age is like learning a new profession, and not of your choosing.'

His daughter waiting for the birth of the baby, telling him:

'Dad, I am alone in this...afraid.'

Yes, no one can scale the limits of the body, they remain permanent.

Father complaining to Mother that we never come close enough to another human being, even in love...

Discussions with Barbara. I was saying that the language that has been established in Australia for writing about the local scene seems quite superficial, little inner life, a sort of cowboy mentality.

If this continues it will create a generation of people who are like this, speak like this, are ashamed of any other approaches or analysis in a desire to belong.

To quote from Jennifer Rutherford's *The Gauche Intruder*:

'Aesthetic objections to Patrick White's style, for example, are heavily coloured by an epistemological ethic in which realism and accessibility of the literary work to the "average reader" becomes synonymous with aesthetic value.'

'The Oz larrikins that have produced a narcissistic enjoyment in an uncouth affability.'

A documentary of Werner Herzog about Klaus Kinski, the actor of his many films. How they met, sharing a boarding house with his mother…his tantrums, excesses and so on…

But what was amazing was that they put on a record of his reading some terrible text about rats, mud and so on, all his tonalities were exactly like Hitler's voice.

A generation that grew up with these types of rhythms, screaming, pretentious stuff.

Miki in the news.

I was telling him before, that *The Visitants* is his most powerful book.

That paragraph about the breakdown: Osana, the old woman, says: 'Alistair said to me, when we were on the veranda, he said:

'"O Naibusi, I think I am going to die. I want to die. I do not want to be mad. I am mad now, Naibusi, and I will not be better. It is like somebody inside me, like a visitor. It is like my body is a house, and some visitor has come, and attacked the person who lived there."

'He said: "O Naibus! O my mother! My house is echoing with the footsteps of the visitor. That person is bleeding. My house is bleeding to death."'

Peggy Glanville-Hicks.

Her opera *Nausicaa* on the radio, introduced by James.

The libretto from a novel by Robert Graves – *Homer's Daughters*. Parts of the opera only broadcast on the ABC.

Teresa Stratas in the main role, unknown at the time.

The opera full of energy, moving music, a combination of main characters singing in English and the chorus in Greek.

Resonances of Greek folkloric music, Church and Byzantine rhythms, but a warm, dramatic ensemble.

Quite high on it.

Why is she not performed more in Australia?

A major composer with more sophistication and depth than a lot of the ones they are giving us.

Thinking of James and Nadine.

Nadine telling me about her father, the musician, who forbade her to see her mother. How she had to lie in order to go and see her.

She was there when he was dying. She said to him: 'I forgive you.'

He was surprised. What had he done to be forgiven...But his last words were: 'I have to go, I will be late for rehearsals...' Absolutely right for a musician.

December

He wrote to ask me for a contribution to a book to be called: *The Public in Australia*.

I tried to write that being a member of the public is in some way a privileged position. One needs or requires a great number of basic skills, such as language, a similar set of values as the larger group, ties of common experience, prejudices of the same type and so on.

A person coming from outside a society is not, for a long time, a member of the public, neither of the local one, nor of the one that they belonged to before, but lies in an in-between place, suspended and uncertain.

This would be the position of most migrants for quite a number of years.

Afternoon coffee at Katerina. She insisted on showing us the enthronement of the Greek Patriarch in Athens that she had recorded some time ago.

The might of the Orthodox Church in view.

The crucified Christ in front of red curtains, the beautiful yellow-red of medieval paintings.

Large icons, all the clergy in white, the deacons in black, the Patriarch in magnificent brocade robes.

An at-ease performance, good voices, arrangements, heads, positions as if coming out of Byzantine paintings, El Greco...

But the most powerful thing was the language, a noble, expansive, lyrical language, the resonance very beautiful to hear...

I was moved, became enthusiastic...

Patriotism, especially of language, is always alive even with the unbelievers...

In Canberra to see the Aboriginal Triennial Exhibition at the National Gallery.

Very good stuff, the animals now in bronze or ceramics, large bronze crocodile with very patterned skin, beautiful light kangaroos in blue and white ceramics, amazingly well caught, so alive, then paintings, the fine detailed strokes...

The huge wall on which other sculpted animals were hung. Bold, amazing work – the grass, the land, stories about kingship,

the Mother Creator...
We were there for a long time.

'One Last Poem'
I was going to write one last poem
but nothing came out,
only lightning & red sand
& a campfire that speaks
at least fifteen Aboriginal dialects
as it stirs the embers with a stick.
Even a whitefella can understand
two or three sentences
if he's prepared to press
his ear to the flames.
The Pintupi have forgotten more than
I'll ever know about the Land –
its ways & names.
Too much to remember,
other than the warning:
don't eat *kuka* in the rain.
'proper cheeky bugger, lightning.'

Today a friend told me,
'everything's a metaphor for something else.'
But what I don't understand is:
why, when I want to describe you, was
the only metaphor that came to mind
the sound of wind blowing in from the desert?
Billy Marshall Stoneking

Journal II

January

The city hot yesterday, with a strong wind and full of flags, flags – something that I dislike – the mark of dictatorship and consumerism.

Chinese proverb:

People who know each other through words are closer than siblings.

Plato:

'Be kind, for everyone you meet is fighting a hard battle. Only the dead have seen the end of the war.'

I think he was born at the beginning of the Peloponnesian Wars, that lasted for a long time.

Missed half of Rostropovich's program conducting the 11th Symphony of Shostakovich.

Very arresting, dark, ominous inner landscapes, powerful, amazing changes of tone.

The Russians, one forgets their passionate power, these watered-down entertainments that we hear now here, and some young musicians that seem at ease in their lack of knowledge and understanding, interested in the new machines and the dead sounds they are producing.

Pasternak invited to the Anti Fascist Congress in Paris in 1935:

'I spoke, I said to them: I understand that this is a meeting of writers to organise resistance to Fascism. I have only one thing to say to you: do not organise. Organisation is the death of art. Only personal independence matters. In 1848, 1917, writers were not organised for or against anything. Do not, I implore you, do not organise.'

Reading Seferis again, his poems, his biography by Roderick Beaton.

'You spoke about things they couldn't see and so they laughed. Yet to row up the dark river against the current, to take the unknown road blindly, stubbornly, and to search for words rooted like the knotted olive tree – let them laugh.

'And to yearn for the other world, to inhabit today's suffocating loneliness, this ravaged present – let them be.'

Some quotes by Plutarch, 46 AD–12 AD, died at Delphi:

'The mind is not a vessel to be filled, but a fire to be kindled.'

'What we achieve inwardly will change outer reality.'

'An in-balance between the rich and the poor is the oldest and most fatal ailments of all republics.'

February

An article in the *New Yorker* about Happiness. The final definition:

'...the state of total immersion in a task that is challenging yet closely matched to one's abilities.'

Simon Rattle and the Birmingham Orchestra on a DVD of twentieth-century music.

John Adams' *Harmonium* – a massive composition with a large orchestra, choirs, on a poem by Dickinson:

Wild nights! Wild Nights!
Were I with thee
Wild night should be
Our Luxury!

Roaming in Eden
Ah! The Sea
Might I but moor – Tonight
in Thee!

An image on TV yesterday reminded me of Rogalsky, the Romanian actor and the children's theatre in Brăila that Mother would take me to see.

That afternoon, Rogalsky as Death, a handsome young man in a long, black velvet cape, coming at dusk to take the soul of the child.

I was so taken with it, that I left my seat, and was hanging at the edge of the stage...

Before, Max in the garden, smelling the voices of the birds all around him in the trees, lifting his head, looking into the trees, closing his eyes as if with a sensual expression. But now, no birds in the trees, no sounds, only the cockatoos that David is feeding.

Elizabeth feeling better – voices – a barometer of our state of being.

In the papers, a young actress saying: Yes, she believes in plastic surgery, she does not want to become a hag.

No one has told her about time and its inexorable advance.

Reading Stendhal's biography by Jonathan Keates: 'Travels to Italy, Florence, a new sense of the visual...The drama of his developing sensibilities dominated this Florentine autumn, yet he found himself lacking either an adequate descriptive language to encompass the experience, or the detachment necessary to record it properly.'

March

Last night watched on NITV a documentary on the efforts to bring an old ceremony to the young, the new generation. *Milpirri: Winds of Change*, and later, part of *Putuparri and the Rainmakers*.

A lament – that the older generation is going, that the young are committing suicide, that the fundamental ceremonies to keep the place alive are not performed, that the whites have been a total corrosive cultural force on the old law.

The need to translate Aboriginal concepts and language into English. One of the elders saying that before you can translate accurately the meaning of words, you must know the culture that gave them meaning. A fundamental thing.

Finally they have to produce a watered down version of the ritual, sacred parts that can not be performed before uninitiated men.

The vast land, the space, the fires at night, the body paintings, the singing, the clapping...all very moving.

'Even if we travel from end to end of every land, nowhere in the world shall we find a country that is alien to us; from everywhere it will be equally possible to raise our eyes to the sky.' Seneca.

How did Eve die, an unacceptable mystery.

On Saturday at JJ for lunch, her two daughters and their husbands there, traces of Eve in their faces, a smile, the colour of their eyes, the movements of their heads.

They were looking at us as if we could take her place. We talked, looked at photos, remembered our travels...only a month and a half since she died, and already life moves forward rapidly.

Came home quite sad.

A documentary on Picabia. Some of his sayings:

'There is only one way out, sacrifice your reputation.'

But for us, who have no reputations, what is the direction?

Later: 'All conviction is a sickness.'

When he died, Marcel Duchamp sent him a telegram:

'Dear Francis, see you soon.'

From Vivienne's papers on ritual, quoting Berger, his depiction of religion as 'a reality maintenance machine'.

Time passing
a silent beat
inside our bones
inexorable.

On television a story from the novel.

The sea, Bondi looking very beautiful, but the people a lot of posturing about passion.

They are like mechanical people that have learned all the positions accurately, imitating all these profiles of seduction, but always fail to create an illusion that they are, that one is dealing with a person who feels.

Quite late – Nacho Duato, the Spanish choreographer – *Jardi Tancat*, the Closed Garden, in Catalan. Music by Maria del Mar Bonet, the score, old Catalan songs.

The dancers, a restrained energy, movements that somehow relate to an inner life, an angularity about them.

Relationships, the implication of the gestures, the interdependency, the inability to survive...

April

Gertrude Stein being interviewed:

'What do you expect of the future?'

'More of the same.'

'What is your attitude to modern art?'

'I like to look at it.'

On the ABC Mairi Nicolson introducing a piece by Saint-Saëns, giving us some information about him. He was involved in a lot of other activities – he wrote books, etc....and then she quoted Berlioz:

'He knows everything, but he lacks inexperience.'

On Sunday we saw Vivienne and Alex's house to be put up for sale. A total transformation, 'decluttered' the new term.

The house spacious now, full of light, empty of things, books, papers...

The light coming in on the polished floors, the staircase. Everything looking elegant.

We were there as if strangers.

But I like empty houses, as if their personalities come up, and they exist on their own, unencumbered by human lives.

The afternoon suddenly full of menace, telephone calls about deaths, operations.

I went on ironing, listening to the radio, a totally tin sound now, nothing but talk-back...endless chitchat and pleasantries, voices of interviewers that are no longer connected to what they express, flowing forward meaninglessly...how lovely, how marvellous, what public response.

Everyone asked for their musical preferences, their favourite romantic music, a sort of community arts...I assume.

I for one, not at all pleased with their new arrangements or tones, a rather false attempt to establish a greater level of intimacy, somehow overstepping the line and not at all effective...

They are going for a cup of tea, their voices inflated and over friendly...

I was telling Alexandra the story about Voltaire.

Voltaire, the anti-cleric is dying. A priest is called to give him the last unction. The priest bends over him and says:

'My son, you must renounce the Devil.'

And Voltaire:

'So late, to make another enemy...'

J reading Dürenmatt, a general article putting forward the idea that art is a struggle with death, that all these energies are going to create something alive, that will last. J stunned at the idea, he never thought of art that way.

May

Celan, in his speech on winning the Bremen Literary Prize in 1958:

'Only one thing that remained reachable, close and secure amid all losses: language.

'Yes, language. In spite of everything, it remained secure against loss. But it had to go through its own lack of answers, through terrifying silence, through the thousand darknesses of murderous speech. It went through. It gave me no words for what was happening but went through it. Went through it and could resurface enriched by it all.'

And later: 'There is nothing in the world for which a poet will give up writing, not even when he is a Jew and the language of his poems is German.'

It Is No Longer
this
Heaviness
lowered at time together with you
into the hour. It is another

It is the weight holding back the void
that would
accompany you.
Like you, it has no name. Perhaps
one day you also will call
me so.

Looking at a documentary on Fassbinder, the German filmmaker. His women, faces as if coming out of drawings by Grosz, an edge of grotesque to them.

One of his lovers that finally committed suicide, was one of the kids born under the Nazi program of 'perfect Aryans'. The place where they brought together perfect blonde women and perfect blonde men to mate, so that they could produce the master race.

But when I was in Berlin, I looked in vain for these ideal specimens, most Berliners seemed to be short and dark...

A review in the *New York Review of Books* of three books by Thomas Bernhard, translated into English. The review by Adam Kirsch.

'But surely Thomas Bernhard is conscious that his attack on dog owners, in *concrete* – sounds manically excessive: "People love animals because they are incapable even of loving themselves. Those with the very basest of souls keep dogs allowing themselves to be tyrannised and finally ruined by dogs...

"It isn't as absurd as it may first appear, when I say that the world owes its most terrible wars to the rulers' love of animals. These people – politicians, dictators – are ruled by a dog..."'

Bernhard in another mood: 'Everything is ridiculous when one thinks of death.'

Last night watched the second Pina Bausch DVD.

A noble, classical line to her choreography, interesting utilisation of the body, of bodies, much more intimate approaches between men and women, sometimes violent, an abstracted violence, even when sexual...and her head very beautiful looking.

The music very effective...Purcell's 'Remember me'...

Wim Wenders who did the film interviewed.

I would have liked more information about her life, her development.

'*Dance, dance, otherwise we are all lost!*'

Pina, some desperation in all the dances...

June

In the afternoon, waiting for them to come, I was looking out of the kitchen window. A plane, like a large fish was gliding through the sky in the soft, afternoon light.

This is the first time I noticed this transformation.

He was cleaning his papers, throwing things out, he thought that I would be interested to see his press cuttings, over many years.

We used to see them daily at the office – arts, culture, all these pronouncements, happenings which at the time seemed so important, now discoloured paper, an amazing example of the futility of current affairs, their emptiness, their exaggeration.

Looking at them you were left with a totally empty feeling.

A black cloud over Athens.

At Olympia they had to light the Olympic flame from electricity, as the sky was covered in black clouds.

And Vasso to Leon: 'Apollo is angry with the people.'

When they come from overseas they make you feel that the centres of power are elsewhere, that this is a backwater. But the landscape is powerful here, and it will bring out interesting, fundamental things, as we become more attuned to it.

Mavis at the funeral of her old friend.

The speakers – a man from the RSL talking with a thin voice, complaining of the cold and the traffic, mispronouncing the name of the dead person...

Mavis: 'The funeral full of people keeling under the weight of medals.'

At the wake – talk, animation, Heathers...

Cold. Heavy rain and lightning during the night. Pouring, as if someone was throwing buckets of water over the house.

Long night. Dark dreams towards morning, in the narrow streets of a city at night.

July

More discussions about the Second World War, the atrocities... Remembered *Shoah*, at the Sydney Film Festival...four hours to show us how common, everyday, acceptable the destruction of people is, how everyone takes it, how the people doing it survive and still look like people.

These terrible, precise, moralistic voices everywhere, self-righteous describing these events, analysing the mechanics of such terrible killings as if they were an office solving-mechanism.

How to get rid of 20,000 people in a week, by the most efficient means.

The letter from the engineer making the gas vans, the balance of the van needed to be reinforced because as the gas came on everyone rushed to the door...

The most everyday analysis of the most terrible killings discussed as if a time and motion study.

Seferis, in a paper called – 'The Latin and The Greek' – 'at the basis of all creative work which is not merely decorative, an exhibit of good taste, or a demonstration of "literary talent", is a single and always similar conflict.

'The conflict arises from a deep-rooted feeling in man that he is immersed in and surrounded by forces which are alien and hostile to his true nature. Something in him aspires towards a personal identity and a liberation which his normal everyday life in the world denies. He desires to be free and self-determinant.

'His art is an expression in visible terms of this invisible and unconscious desire.'

Alex in hospital feeling better. Today he was high on his first shower, he felt like a large salmon in oil.

Alex's comparative points are always culinary.

Listening to T.S. Eliot last night, in the DVD, propounding that we have a few ideas in a lifetime...as if he was not writing from inner experience, a shifting field, lights that fall on an inner landscape and illuminate some part of it with a new understanding.

On Friday night we went to the Balmain Town Hall to hear the poetry reading.

We waited on comfortable chairs, young women coming to offer us wine and entrees.

Next to Jurgis a young woman, very young.

Jurgis began a conversation with her.

'Are you a poet too?'

The girl: 'A beginner.'

'How did you drift into poetry?'

'Seeing *Shakespeare in Love*.'

At least something converts them to poetry.

An interview with Moravia about *The Conformist*, the film of his novel, Bertolucci present too.

That frightening, brutal film about the actual selling of one's soul.

The film – perfect images, the landscape, the elegance of women, the interiors, and then the brutal murder in the forest...

They were discussing Pirandello, apparently his birthplace at the most southern tip of Italy, colonised by the Greeks, was originally called *KAOS*, the name of the Taviani Brother's film of the Pirandello stories.

Looking at these social occasions in which writers behave as if part of the cocktail scene, and yet are supposed to come up with truths that would not be palatable, accessible, wild, so to speak, in terms of that audience.

Everyone telling anecdotes about each other…how great everyone is…all a very commercial undertaking…

Mishima, in the interview describing the Japanese character in terms of – Elegance and Brutality.

Remembered the first time I heard about *harakiri*.

Winter, at home in Brăila, the house warm and full of light. Snow outside, Mother and Father preparing to go and see a French film with Charles Boyer playing a Japanese navy officer committing harakiri.

The evening very vivid in my memory.

In the paper an article about Man Ray, Kiki and the black mask. On his tomb in Montparnasse, his epitaph reads: 'Unconcerned but not indifferent.'

August

In Search of Happiness, a book by John H. Schumaker, reviewed in the paper – small, critical, sceptical approach.

A quote from the book: Leonardo da Vinci: 'Simplicity is the ultimate sophistication.'

Looking again at David Brooks's essay published in the eighties – 'Poetry and Sexual Difference'.

His essays intellectually stimulating, but not confrontational, a warm, human tone of someone searching in all these rooms full of intellectual theories, approaches to literature, differences between men and women...a young voice, still full of hope.

Domestic dream.

In the kitchen. Mother by the sink. I, holding Max in my arms. His fur golden brown, opening his green-yellow eyes from time to time.

I: 'Max what is the meaning of all this purring?'

And Max, in a male voice: 'No meaning at all.'

We are all cleaning our gardens, pruning, feeding, watering. The weather marvellous, dry and warm.

Yesterday, I could hear some of the sparrows coming back.

At the opening, we arrived late, the whole place full. For the first time a feeling of warmth in the air.

She, as usual, looking polite, warm and detached at the same time, in black, with that astonishing colouring of her skin, as if gold-dusted, and her red-golden hair, dyed, but somehow totally suited to the effect.

But he, scraggy, his curly hair shooting out of his skull as if a medusa, his eyes very black with some desperation that he was trying to keep in check, his glass in hand, running after the waiter to pour him another drink.

He was rushing trying to escape these fires that were coming at him from everywhere...laughing in a forced yet careless way...

Her paintings – large, sombre...an inner calligraphy in dark browns, black blues...

Re-reading Bulgakov – *The Master and Margarita* – very well sustained, a human yet terrible cutting irony.

The Devil – always well dressed, with good manners, bringing foods of an exotic kind…at a time in Russia when food was difficult to get, starvation in real life.

But the whole thing so well sustained, taking you in, his dialogue, the freedom of the scenes as if totally cleared of encumbrances – allowed to float…

September

At night, listening to the old songs in the silence of the kitchen.

All these passionate voices that I had forgotten about, that brought with them, vaguely, other times in my life when they were related to some immediate feeling in me, friends… affections…now gone…

Things that at the time were important, some inner involvement that I had forgotten about and that the music brought with it…echoes, slightly unplaced…

An interview with Elizabeth Jane Howard, Kingsley Amis' second wife – the difficulties of life with him…a writer herself, her closing remarks:

'The most important things in life can not be taught; they have to be found out by yourself. But life is so organised that you get the hang of things just when you're on the way out.

It seems frightfully unfair.'

Oscar Wilde:

'To regret one's experience is to arrest one's own development. To deny one's own experience is to put a lie into the lips of one's life.'

Last night on the terrace, the planes far away in the night sky, going towards the airport, small birds flickering in the air.

The lights on the Anzac Bridge, a row of yellow small explosions. I was thinking – a lot of people that gave me substance have gone…a diminished presence…lighter and lighter…when we too will disappear.

Morton Feldman, American avant-garde composer, 'Conversations without Stravinsky': 'From this he deduces (Kafka in *The Castle*) that rules are for those who rule. What they do is rule.

'This is why all my knowledge does not make me understand what Mozart did that I should do, in order to reach a state of artistic grace.

'The composer's dilemma seems inseparable from the medium itself. He dreams of a music that will transcend the instruments and still remain magnificently idiomatic. To achieve this dream he naturally turns to the technical material at hand.'

The same with language, trying to transcend it, yet use it to say something real.

Listening to Saint-Saëns – *Samson and Delilah* – suddenly Calas came in singing the magnificent aria – *Mon coeur s'ouvre à ta voix* – a rich, dark, noble interpretation, rising upwards – I was stunned. This is what we must aim for.

October

At Barbara's for dinner. One of Harry's friends there. Born in Turkey, he said, ISMIR...SMYRNA...

I remembered how we stopped at the harbour on our way to Greece from Romania, ate very beautiful, golden grapes – Kadaif, the special sweet which I had never had before...

Seferis, his native city that he left when he was an adolescent, visited it in the sixties, I think, all their family homes, childhood, gone, now a city of some millions, from the small place of his childhood.

Dream towards morning.

At some social gathering, everyone discussing newly published books. This woman next to me asking if I am having a book published. I:

'Hopefully at the end of the year, next year...'

And she, in this terrible saccharine voice:

'In multiple copies?'

Some irony there.

For the last few weeks, this large, black bird, in the pine tree, making the harshest of sounds, on and on, as if laments, every few minutes.

All the neighbours driven to distraction by it.

We tried to define it, was it love or loss, we decided on love, seeing it is spring.

It has gone now, but still comes from time to time calling to some other friends in the park, far away.

Looking at a DVD of Tarkovsky's *The Stalker*, on the small screen the chilliness of the environment doesn't quite come off. But the philosophical discussions do, the inner journey, the despair of the Stalker that no one believes in anything any longer.

The entire zone a very dark, destroyed environment full of unpredictable forces changing with every inner attempt.

A tortured place, actually with no life, only a black dog, young and quite lively.

And the wife with the maimed daughter, who can't walk...
A vision of the present. A vision of the future.

At night, I watched again *Les Enfants du Paradis*, still very moving.

It survives, it engages, it convinces. Prévert's script very good, a strong line.

The actors – Arletty and Barrault, full of innocence, lightness, like a flight of gestures.

Marcel Carné made it in 1945, at the time of the war, more than seventy-five years ago.

Beautifully shot in black-and-white.

Jim's photos of Uluru, the blue of the sky with a flank of the rock, a liquidity about it, as if a human limb.

A documentary on Olive Cotton.

Her photographs very beautiful, subtle, her whites, very ethereal, as if an imaginary white...by comparison – Dupain, more energy perhaps, while hers a floating quality of light...

November

The House of Exile, Evelyn's book. The life and times of Heinrich Mann and Nelly Kroeger-Mann.

Very good, unusual in its treatment of history, a panoramic view yet anchored in very good details that give it immediacy... The enormous task of putting together all that research, information crossing each other and finding a tone at once intimate and scholarly with ease and elegance.

She wears her scholarship lightly.

An article by Jonathan Rée about Søren Kierkegaard and Hans Christian Andersen. Kierkegaard's analysis of Andersen's novels:

'Andersen's novels do not perform the kind of transubstantiation of experience that one expects from a great work of art, and they lack that deeper unity which allows a novel to have the centre of gravity itself.'

Miki has died.

His small, careful writing. He always responded like a well-behaved child to the letters, the books I sent him.

A miracle that he survived so long with all his inner difficulties.

A lonely, wounded person. An ice in him that he never found an antidote for, nothing could melt it.

Yet, when you saw his eyes, very blue and full of exploding blue fire.

Very, very sad.

Did he have any friends in that small town by the sea? When I asked him, he spoke only of books, antiquarians and pubs.

Andrew has died too. They rang to tell me.

This simplicity of dying. Suddenly, something no longer works inside and the whole edifice collapses.

His body on the bathroom floor for a few hours, going cold, and he absent – totally now.

To cheer myself watched the DVD of the *Total Balalaika Show*, Aki Kaurismäki, the Leningrad Cowboys and the Alexandrov Red Army Chorus and Dance Ensemble in Helsinki's Senate Square, June 1993.

But last night, in spite of the jollity, the music, the singers and so on, a rather sad night – thinking of the first time I saw it, at the State Theatre during the Sydney Film Festival, with Gweneth and Adrian, I, as usual making a great deal of noise, enthusiastic, laughing too loud, the people in front getting angry with me...

But now everyone dead...Jurgis who discovered Kaurismäki, Gweneth, Adrian, and so on...

December

More mines in the North.

The land photographed from a helicopter, this beautiful, warm, brown-red expanse that they are hacking at, the skin of the earth that we are continuously cutting away, the mines, like wounds on the ground.

We are bent on selling, taking no notice of people, animals, plants.

But what about the Aboriginal people, is anyone asking them

about all this? They seem to live mostly in poverty and probably die of desperation and in silence...only the noise of the whites is heard, demanding more and more...

Auden coming from America to Oxford University, he did not want to hear discussions about dreams:

'The subconscious is inherently boring.'

His assessment.

They insisted that I must come and see the film with them. I reluctant, but had to go.

In the theatre they had blown up the film to cinemascopic proportions, and the soundtrack as if for deaf people. Everything is getting bigger and bigger, more simplistic and fit for the plastic personalities that go for empty sounds. They will finally come to pump up the chickens, and the apples, and the bread, and everything else to bring them to the required size that will match this inflated image of the world which the machines are increasingly giving us...

He was talking about Erasmus's anniversary, this great man, this genius, adored by half of Europe, Kings that wanted him at their courts etc., etc....

Erasmus must have been quite tough to have taken all this adulation and remained himself, survived inwardly.

An Italian film about two nuclear physicists – *The Atom Men* [*Di ragazzi di via Panisperna*]. Their view: 'All knowledge is suspended above an abyss. We only discover what we want to discover.'

We must simply go on with whatever we consider essential in ourselves, and not be distracted by all this noise around us.

Henry Moore's figures in the landscape, something so reassuring. I remembered his exhibition at the art gallery, very beautiful, noble, human forms, monumental, yet intimate.

The drawings, the etchings, the use of gouache in whites, reds, greens, amazingly delicate.

The large, razor-edged figure in movement, the same feeling as the Greek sculptures, a wind moving through it.

The whole exhibition an inspiration and encouragement to see what he achieved after sixty, how he worked continuously, ten years for some forms to emerge, in inner terms ten years is nothing, the thing inside will take its time to come to fruition and the only thing one can do is work at it.

This inner work, and then the capability of finding a stylistic expression for it, the most tenuous of things.

The high-rise apartments are cracking.

As U used to say:

'The material never forgets.'

The conclusions of a civil engineer.

At the Opera House, the light sparkled on the waters, the boats moved like heavy monsters under the bridge, and Rossini's *La Cenerentola*.

Rossini the magician!

Music full of light, virtuosity, all taken in with enormous grace and lack of heaviness.

Later I bought a DVD of the opera with Francisco Araiza and Frederica von Stade in the title roles.

An interesting production and the two matched vocally, a marvellous chemistry between them, at ease, warm, von Stade, an innocence that not only conquered Araiza, but us as well.

In the last part, von Stade, as if a river of music flowing through her throat full of light, golden colours...all the vocal difficulties of the score totally forgotten.

In an interview with Araiza:

'I am a person who depends very much on colleagues...'

The interviewer:

'What if you have to sing Cenerentola with a singer that you don't like?

Araiza:

'I close my eyes and think it is Flicka von Stade...but when I open them...'

They both laugh.

Reading about Rossini. He wrote the opera when he was twenty-five, in a few weeks, but he had been writing since he was fifteen.

He lived his last years in France, he left money for prizes 'to be given to writers who observe the laws of morality, which modern writers completely ignore.'

This in 1868.

Journal III

January

Jolanta last night, talking about the past, the war, escaping Lithuania after the Russian takeover. They travelled on foot, on carts, on trains towards the West. Reached Germany. American and English planes were coming to bomb, they were so low that you could see the markings on the planes.

A terrible fear got hold of her, she turned white, stiff, began to run, does not remember anything about it...her Mother told her of the transformations...she must have been fourteen at the time.

Running all of them towards a bunker, the planes spraying bullets, finally reaching it...coming back to herself, but the people in the bunker did not want to open the door, finally they did...

Then Mother having a heart attack. Lying as if already dead. Terrible headaches, Jolanta putting cold compresses on her forehead...

Time, as if no longer continuous, as if it had totally stopped...

Somehow being permanently fixed there...for nearly a day. Suddenly realising that one can feel outside time...

Before me longing
and behind me fate
Umar Ibn al-Farid 1181–1235, celebrated Arab poet.

A message from the past found among old papers:

The Fire Ring

In the rain of heat
the pavements burnt
the walls, sheets of white fire.

I walked, small, holding on to his hand.
The streets he walked were still unknown
to me, I was on safer ground.

'I know,' he said, 'that the wild fire at
the core can not be shared, it is not to be
shared, refuses to be shared with anyone.
Do you follow me?' I tried to force
my way against the light
that came in scorching waves.

'The ring is sacred ground, try and
understand, it lives within its years
outside of time,
moves like a burning river sheltered
by high walls, trap walls, petrified
by centuries of fear.'

Walls, he said, that can be shattered
only once, never to grow again.
I watched him, unaware then
and so helpless
practice the breakthrough
like an addict, intent, possessed.

February

Chitra speaking of the well-known writer. They will probably kill him with so much attention, adulation.

She has revised her view of him, he is not a genius being led astray and away from his true path, but a writer of limited possibilities who has decided to be famous...and he is succeeding very well.

In Canberra with JJ, not feeling well at all, the feeling that I had last year when I got lost in the bush above K's house.

On top of the hill, the wind silent through the trees, the house seemingly far down, unrecognisable, no marks that I could pick in the landscape, everything looked the same.

The impression of a fatal loss. Dry, blonde grass everywhere, blind rabbits sitting in the bush.

Dusk...

The current Russian composers that we have not heard at all, or very little – Gubaidulina, Kancheli...

A documentary on Alfred Schnittke, sombre, moving music with an embracing emotional undercurrent.

Who was he? His mother German and a Catholic, most of her children sent to labour camps.

He seemed to be part of a community of musicians, critics... One critic was telling us that the change in his music came with his mother's death...he became more compassionate.

'Compassion,' he said, 'requires a more melodic line.'

Religious music, amazing utilisation of women's voices.

Three Sacred Hymns. The Faust Cantata.

Then he had a stroke, he partially lost consciousness – he saw himself as a child and was very cold...

'It must have been in the north,' he said.

He has a very humane, lived face, speaking of deep, serious things, as if an intrinsic part of his life.

He was trying to grasp things that are difficult to express, he felt that music is nearer to this possibility, a feeling, a suggestion – bringing it together to catch the mystery of living, of dying.

The title of the documentary: *Words Return to Music – The Unreal World of Alfred Schnittke.*

Nikos is having an exhibition in Vienna. He will send a catalogue, I was thinking of the early opening at Barry Stern's.

In the silence of the gallery his fruit waited against a brooding metaphysical background. These magnificent shapes absolutely as if made of volumes of colour, colour with an amazing solidity, yet light, the two quinces, the cherries, the pears...The most amazing, rich, yet explosive colour.

A beautiful balanced group.

In spite of so many invitations sent out, only friends came. And no sales.

March

Mother and Balzac...the involvement, living with the characters, the astonishment at Balzac's force, style, ability to make things alive, provincial lives, the extremes of human passion.

Mother and Stendhal...*Le Rouge et le Noir*...all that subtle analysis of love, the Revolution, after the Revolution...

And last night, looking at this not very interesting film of the life of a man finally killed at the guillotine.

He had written his memoirs, he was being visited in prison by Prosper Mérimée.

All these names from the past with no currency here, that are always attacking me suddenly, and no one to talk to about all this.

With Jolanta to see the old jazz films – Bessie Smith – 'St Louis Blues', her voice, the voice of the chorus around her, their faces, an all-black cast, very powerful and moving. But Hollywood was obviously not interested in these forms.

In the Lena Horne film, an all-black musical – *Stormy Weather* – all this sentimental get up with a thousand girls in pompons, a choreography to make one cry or laugh. In this terrible environment there was Lena Horne, a beautiful, noble, elegant woman with a magnificent voice.

If one could strip all the sentimental excesses of Hollywood, racism – they constantly thought that they must be made to look, to sound, to behave like the whites – they could have been at ease as themselves.

Still, in spite of that they managed to throw off some of the images.

The dancers as well, amazing tapping, the Nicholas Brothers, energy, elegance, lightness, improvisation, enormous verve, yet no one has heard of them, by comparison – Fred Astaire – looks both tame and sentimental.

Speaking of her latest book, she is very pleased with it, she stripped the characters right down, she wanted them to go through these terrible experiences, horrific experiences...

A new thing for her.

Dinner at Double Bay for Indra's birthday. Indra looking well, sparkling darkly with her earrings, her black silk top, and everyone in a good mood.

Then we went to Rushcutters Bay for coffee at her flat. The lighted houses on the hill in the black humidity of the night. The water full of rich blue-grey reflections, the surface of the water as if melted metal.

Giacometti:

'What is important is to create an object capable of conveying a sensation as close as possible to the one felt at the sight of the subject.'

How curious it is reading Pavese's journals, *Le Metier de Vivre*. How could one translate the title...The Trade of Living...The Craft of Living...

You have no inkling what was going on inside him. This constant transformation, this hiding of what we feel or fear into analytical thought, comparative points, literary analogies and so on.

I assume to diminish the potency of events.

It is as if you are reading of a parallel person to Pavese.

Culling letters, papers, again and again, so much excessive

material. But it all seems difficult, as if the material too has its own periphery of existence and resents being denied its space.

April

The autumn cry of birds above the park, the milky transparency of the air above the trees, diffused in the morning sunlight. A resonance now from far away, now near, urgent, repetitive.

Elizabeth – the painting has been finished, the house looks very good, elegant from outside, especially, and some of the inside rooms have been painted too.

A lighter, more vulnerable feeling to her voice.

The selling of the house, as if the event brought her into some other area…all these transformed realities constantly posing changes in one's immediate life.

Adaminaby – cold, misty mountains, with beautiful golden autumn trees, the colour so vivid as if artificial.

At Hyams for Alex's birthday. The sea very silent and still. At night, a full moon on the waters, the light raining luminous on top of the still surface…raining from an unknown source, the moon, somehow too high up to serve as the source. Travelling back through Canberra we went to Parliament House. The wind still blowing on the hill, rattling the metal poles as if bones in the wind.

Beautiful drive back, the sun on the short grasses, fields made

of ginger-red fur, blonde fur, and the trees around flaming red...
In Goulburn – a coffee at the Paragon Cafe.

We went with Mavis to see *Ginger and Fred*, Fellini's latest film. Gwen and Adrian were there. We sat together.

The film, baroque, magnificently funny and satirical, a total indictment of television and advertising, this listening to music while talking, the television sets everywhere, underlying our lives, the world made of televisions, full of an assortment of freaks.

James at the Adelaide Festival watching a performance of Shakespeare's *Richard III* by the Rustaveli Theatre Company. Describing the effect on him, the music, the sounds, the actors, an elderly company. While here everyone ignores the mature person...they all go for the young, young and empty. The play in Georgian, if the actors would have started to speak in English, no one would have noticed, because, somehow they all took Georgian in.

As he came out of the theatre, he was ten feet off the ground.

A book on Lucian Freud's exhibition of drawings, etchings. Some of his remarks:

'You are very conscious of the air going around people in different ways, to do with their particular vitality.

'I am interested in people as animals. Part of liking to work from the nude is for that reason.

'Art has always had to do with sensuality and selfishness. My work is autobiographical. It's like a diary.

'I work with people that interest me, that I care about, in rooms I live in and I know.

‘With etching there’s an element of danger and mystery. You don’t know how it is going to come out.

‘What’s black is white, what’s left is right.’

May

A documentary on Margaret Thatcher. England’s influence on world affairs, her vision of patriotism, a combination of economic benefits, the most illusory of measures. No other definition of life.

Looking at her, and all the politicians, everyone sustained by a historic setting in which they imagine their gestures too will acquire a historic dimension, but these poor, wooden halls, what can they add to them?

What everyone is selling via a lot of advertisements, hairdos, black cars, houses in the country, tone of voice, is some limited illusion.

In the whole analysis of Thatcher, no one touches on the question of class.

Most of her cabinet made up of lords.

She spoke constantly of betrayal, assassins with a smile, after all she had done for them, keeping them in power for so long.

Listening to Berlioz – *Romeo et Juliette* – with the Paris Opera conducted by Barenboim.

A lament, a lament, beautifully developed but very sad.

Dark tones, then changes into lighter ones, haunting passages, snippets as if of memory.

The soloists – very brief passages.

Angelopoulos – *The Suspended Step of the Stork* – a sad, moving film.

These crumbling old houses, things and lives that are going under the brutal impact of events.

The scenes of the wedding on both sides of the river, people separated, beautiful and understated, in fact the whole film understated…borders…people kept out…

The last images of the electricity men going up to install the cables of communication…higher and higher, in their yellow-orange plastic suits, suspended on the poles as if dancers, people coming up for air, higher in the sky, a religious feeling of higher aspirations, longings, all underlined by Eleni Karaindrou's moving music.

June

Glenn Gould in the documentary about him:

'A concert is not a bullfight, but a love relationship with the audience.'

Tamara sent an email that Alexandra had arrived:

The lilacs
are in bloom
in Riga

On Thursday night woke up coughing, afraid that I would wake up someone in the house.

I suddenly realised that there was no one there but me.

All gone to places of no return, and I alone in the empty house, the total silence and the rain falling softly.

Remarks about the *Sydney Journals*. Jim very enthusiastic about the book, he felt that the bulbul was my totem bird. He looked for it in his bird book, described as if coming from Asia, an outsider, not a native, came into Sydney and the suburbs. Described in the book as: 'It felt commodious in the suburbs.'

The Dream.

We were running together down this dark street, no lights, but the feeling was that we were in a small town well known to us, safe.

And suddenly, as we reached a small square, by some magic, à la Bulgakov, I was up on this statue in the middle of the square, trying to hold on to a ledge that was coming off. The statue made of brown marble breaking at my touch as if made of chalk.

I was stunned. How did it happen? I looked down at the square for some help. Suddenly at the bottom of the statue this tall man was standing looking at me and smiling.

At ease. He looked like Bulgakov in one of his early photographs, but he was dressed as if for a performance – Molière, I thought, in grey silk, a seventeenth-century court dress and buckled shoes.

I turned my head to the statue trying to hold on to its head. The statue was of a middle-aged man, in a self-important, heroic mode, with his hair parted on one side.

At my touch, the top of his head broke off. I tried to put it back, but now it only fitted back to front.

Suddenly I was in the street. I looked up relieved, to see that from below the damage was not evident.

And then I was running again with this short man who was carrying his dry-cleaning and talking about the architecture of the town.

July

Karl Shapiro on poetry:

'Poetry is no more language than landscape is paint.'

He went to see her, amazed at the total messiness of the place. Quite stunned in fact, that anyone could live like this. He felt that the objects were taking over and that somehow she could not defend herself against them...

Nina going into Ola's house after her death. How terrible it was to come into the house without her there, look into her things, trying to clear things out.

Lots of photographs of me.

Thinking of the house, empty now, when we visited, we had the front bedroom, hearing footsteps on the pavement outside as one lay in bed.

The room full of books, Polish souvenirs, rugs on the walls, suitcases everywhere marked with some passage through unknown countries...Russia, Persia...New Zealand.

The nights full of dark dreams, people, and running...

In the night, a boat at the edge of the waters, this pontoon that moved towards us, like a plank across the waters, moved by chains that were sounding in the night.

I was suddenly afraid, but the woman next to me said: 'Don't be afraid, just get on and don't look at the waters.' In a moment we were inside the boat, we were paying for our tickets, the money full of the subtle colours, as those of Henry Moore's sketches at the Art Gallery.

'She fell in love in such an epic way,' they were saying. And she, growing old, looking at these amazing transformations in us, that none of us could believe were happening.

Witnesses to the most dangerous and fundamental transformations that will take us away with them, were asking:

'Is this death?'

Death
as if pruning
near us
then further out
then back, close.

August

How to define Cavafy – in the streets, living in his fashion, human, ironic, resigned, warm at times, always a soft spot for young men, understanding of human trespasses, but not too humble about it, definitely in love with Hellenism.

Reading in the *Guardian* an article by F. Gibbons about Jean-Luc Godard. An interview with him, eighty now, proposing an ingenious solution to Europe's financial crisis, especially Greece's.

'The Greeks gave us logic. We owe them for that. It was Aristotle who came up with the big "therefore" as in..."You don't love me anymore...therefore..." Or, "I found you in bed with another man... therefore..."

'We use this word millions of times to make our most important decisions. It's about time we started paying for it.

'If every time we use the word "therefore" we have to pay 10 euros to Greece, the crisis will be over in one day and the Greeks will not have to sell the Parthenon to the Germans. We have the technology to track all these therefores on Google.

'We can even bill people by phone.

'Every time Angela Merkel tells the Greeks, we lent you this money, therefore you must pay us back with interest, she must first pay them their royalties.'

An ingenuous solution, but who will take it up?

Cold. The wind blowing. Sharp light as in late autumn. Birds, great emptiness and silence everywhere, only from time to time people walking their dogs and in the garden, the young Indian mynas running through the grass, the wind blowing their feathers, glossier than those of their parents.

Finished reading Dennis's *Standing Still*. Well sustained, bitterly witty, desperate, catching well the terrible repetitive elements.

He managed to sustain the tone throughout, with a few

lapses, an enormous stylistic leap from the last piece of prose I read ten years ago.

I was very pleased that all of us are working, developing, achieving something.

Woke up late. I wondered where Max was to give him his food. He was on the terrace going through the feathered remains of a pigeon, searching for any tidbits left, smelling them one by one, in case he had been careless...

WELL!

I went on protesting and he searching the debris.

To the cemetery on Sunday. The early streets empty, windy. Finally the bus came and we went slowly on our long run. Greeks in the bus going to the cemetery, like me. Watching them I had forgotten all these gestures, talk, expressions. The women's voices very high, sharp, as if wind in the high trees in winter.

The same woman selling flowers in the shop, that I had seen for so many years, slightly older now, like myself.

All the flowers had dried out on the grave.

The sky very, very blue. A plane suspended, as if painted on the surface of the blue, above the tombs on the hill.

Very tired inwardly, thinking constantly of the many things I have to do, everything seems an imposition.

Yesterday, I stayed inside and watched arts programs.

Akhmatova, a Russian film celebrating one hundred years since her birth. Anatoly Naiman interviewed, the very interesting writer, describing Akhmatova, the communist period. Language had become totally polluted, unreal, clogged with terrible things, like a sewer, he said, flowing over all things, and in the middle of this terrible current, Akhmatova, a small stone, covered, battered by all this but maintaining its nature, holding on to essentials.

September

Angelopoulos and *Ulysses' Gaze*. His cinematic, visual sense remains masterly and his deep involvement in fundamental issues. The immediacy of the killings in Sarajevo, the destruction of all these European cities, and then, the actual places we had left in Romania.

Constanta, the Black Sea and the street, that I still remember, going upwards before it falls into the sea.

Looking at all these places where we waited for the boat to take us to Greece.

Finally Brăila, my home town. He did not show much of it, some church spires in the distance, the restaurant by the Danube where we used to go in summer, where the boats from Galatz used to come, from where we went with the school, at the end of the war, on an excursion, and saw half of the city burnt down by the Germans on their retreat.

At the end of the film, the giant statue of Lenin, travelling down the river.

They rang to tell me that Costas had died...not fifty yet.

I remembered him in the camp, going back to our respective

huts after the dance. Tall, dark, very good-looking, and a good dancer. But I was totally outside the line of his future life, his imagined future life, I was already burdened with our many problems.

Later, after he married, he kept following me from the university, proposing things quite unethical in view of his wife at home with their first child.

He had already transformed within a few years, the language of a libertine now, later, undoubtedly, he would become more careless, rougher.

October

The melancholy produced by information bulletins, more books, more prizes, the discovery of another genius...

While I am sitting in the kitchen, the door open, strong sunlight and Max in the shade.

The roses pushing out and no horizon that I can see...

Some quotes from La Rochefoucauld to cheer us a little:

'Everyone complains of their memory, but no one complains of their judgement.'

'There is "true love" as there is apparition of spirits, everyone talks about them, but few have seen them.'

'The most violent passions leave us free from time to time, but vanity – troubles us always.'

She arrived an hour late, with flowers.

Very pale skin and dark eyes, very dark hair, slightly dyed, but discreetly.

Everything about her glossy, from her black watch with diamonds, for night vision, to her rings, bracelets, leather bag, mobile, heavy leather jacket...a person of means...

'Multiskilled', this is how she described herself.

She talked a lot, unnerved by us watching her performance, was looking for a job, her English good, but with interesting sudden flashes. Discussing something. she was 'negatively impressed' or 'impressed negatively'.

These messages from the old country, it is as if they are bringing another, foreign image of it, less warm, less at ease. They all have a hungry aspect, inwardly hungry, some impatience to reach a point of satiety, the feeling forced on them by such terrible political circumstances.

Max and the Magpie.

Max in the garden in the sun. The Magpie comes down as usual to examine the grass, carefully.

Suddenly it becomes aware of Max, walks slowly on its thin legs to the other side of the lawn, watching Max constantly, while Max watches her constantly.

Finally they face each other across the path, they eye each other silently.

The Magpie crosses over but away from Max, walks with a nonchalant air, sums up the situation, but keeps away, at a reasonable distance, what is supposed to be the other's territory, not infringing on it.

Max gets up and goes to the water dish, drinks from it, the

Magpie is now on the gate, looking out at other possibilities in the street. Then it flies away.

Max changes position, out of the sun, near the mandarin tree. Everything done in a polite and reasonable silence, the movements, the assessment behind them.

November

In an old *New York Review of Books*, a review by James Fenton of the life of Joseph Cornell – the man with the art boxes.

'Although Cornell was by no means averse to success, in principle, he could only sample it in homeopathic doses.'

I rather like that.

Louise Glück's latest volume of poetry, *A Village Life*.

I have always liked her poetry, her tone, her approach, the insights she is able to make tangible.

There is an energy in her, a savage energy that I find totally appropriate – the 'Mock Orange' poem, she reading it, that has remained constantly with me.

But the current book, not only a sad and discouraged tone to the poems, but the conclusions about life.

Nature, very much present, sometimes as an obsessive presence.

The cover suggests that it is somewhere in Europe, but to me totally American.

On TV astrophysicists and theologians talking about God and the universe. All these theoretical positions that they are checking...

foolproof…and then, in fifty years they can all see that they were measuring their own hypothetical assumptions.

At the party this navy captain was telling us that each vessel has a signature sound that can be distinguished from any other, and that this signature sound can be picked up and used – in warfare… etc.…

Even though you are dealing with the same machinery, the same parts, when they come together they form a specific body, that becomes recognisable as an entity, a personality…

A documentary by Ken Burns, the very good American documentary-maker, this time on the rise of Huey Long, as Governor of Louisiana.

Before his arrival, the place described as having one major crop – Dissent –

The crow yesterday, a harsh, lamenting sound, powerful in the pine tree, changing keys, throwing these short guttural sounds to the tree, the air, whoever was listening.

These heavy sounds out of this small body.

December

Very, very hot yesterday, 38 degrees. That glassy stillness over the city, the streets. Going out, the air as if coming out of an overheated oven. The nights depressingly hot and somehow humid.

Reading about an earlier attack by the Americans on a city in Iraq. The operation called: *Phantom Fury*.

They must have surrealist writers devising the names of these battles.

A program on Middle Europe, on Romania this time.

The Kings – Carol, Michael as a young person, then Carol's abdication. Michael and his mother, war, communism...

The re-runs of these terrible events, these political dictatorships, these fiascos that people had to pay for, these ideas of how they were going to serve the people, and then, they all transform into the same greedy, indifferent, hard, self-serving megalomaniacs.

The rapidity with which people clap in unison, bow in unison...

In hospital after the operation, I woke up surrounded by curtains. I did not know how devastated I would be. No energy, sick with all the smells, terrible food. Everything tastes like disinfectant.

Everyone came to visit, brought flowers, fruit, rang, the sound of the telephone oppressive, no energy to answer.

But everyone here nice, we are all waiting for our bodies to heal – hope that the tests will not bring future disasters.

The place with a tempo of its own, like a large city, young people doing their duties, all polite, Asian students finishing their degrees.

The proximity and danger of the situation making for more intimate exchanges with unknown people, exchanges of views, confessions about our lives.

Lisa, the person in the cubicle next to mine, from New Zealand, discussions about the country.

At night, walking in the corridors past rooms with people asleep.

The night outside, views of the hospital ground, the university's tennis courts, few people passing, birds flying in the strong lights above the park, white birds transparent in the night.

Trying to sleep, the curtains drawn around us, the sound of the machines, like a soft beat in the night.

From the next cubicle Lisa's breathing...I suddenly thought of Rilke's lines:

You, neighbour God, if sometimes in the night
I rouse you with loud knocking, I do so
only because I seldom hear you breathe;
I know: You are alone.
And should you need a drink, no one is there
to reach it to you, groping in the dark.
Always I hearken. Give but a small sign.
I am quite near.

Vrasidas giving a talk at the university. The wife of a Member of Parliament had come wearing a lot of heavy jewellery. Vrasidas remembered an essay by Diderot in which the jewels were using the human body to show themselves off.

He said something to that effect to her, and she: 'I am afraid professor that I don't understand you.'

Vrasidas knocks them with these sources of scholarly information – floats above the narrow issues, to produce some wit.

Reading again Isaiah Berlin's – 'Meeting with Russian Writers in 1945 and 1956', an essay I read in the early eighties and now included in a book of his essays, *Personal Impressions*. The whole article marvellous in its ability to evoke meetings with Akhmatova, Pasternak and other Russian writers at the time.

An approach that tries at all times to tread very delicately, maintain a balance between his enthusiasm, the personalities of the writers and a constant desire to present them as close to their truth as possible.

The article starts with a long introduction, for the English reader, of the literature of Russia in the last fifty years or so, major figures, Pasternak, who at the time was writing *Dr Zhivago*, Akhmatova writing *The Requiem*, others already gone – Mandelstam, Tsvetaeva, Mayakovsky...

On Akhmatova:

'She spoke of the dark undercurrents of their lives, of fear.

'She had begged to be allowed to translate the letters of Rubens, not those of Romain Rolland...finally they gave her permission.

'I asked whether the Renaissance was a real historical past to her, inhabited by imperfect human beings, or an idealised image of an imaginary world.

'She replied that it was, of course, the latter; all poetry and art to her was – here she used an expression once used by Mandelstam – a form of nostalgia, a longing for a universal culture, as Goethe and Schlegel had conceived of it, of what has been transmuted into art and thought – of nature, love, history, nothing outside itself.

'She spoke in a calm, even voice, like a remote princess in exile, proud, unhappy, unapproachable, often in words of the most moving eloquence.'

On Pasternak:

'He spoke in magnificent, slow moving periods, with occasional intense rushes of words; his talk often overflowed the banks of grammatical structure, lucid passages were succeeded by wild, but always marvellously vivid and concrete images.

'These might be followed by dark words, when it was difficult to follow him, and then he would suddenly come into the clearing again.

'The only person who seems to me to have talked as he talked was Virginia Woolf, who to judge from the few occasions on which I met her, made one's mind race as he did and obliterated one's normal vision of reality in the same exhilarating, at times, terrifying way.'

Penelope Fitzgerald interviewed by Murray Waldren:

'With astonishing detail and deceptively simple narrative Fitzgerald builds little time-fused stories that continue to explode with insights long after you have finished reading them. And always there is that mischievous wit and delicate irony.'

She responds:

'I don't see how we can avoid irony if you are going to get through the day at all. I would very much like to write without it, but that's difficult in English. Almost no one can do it except D.H. Lawrence who didn't mind exposing himself to people laughing at him. But normally we seek to protect ourselves, and irony is self-protection...

'It is a very British trait, but what else can one do?

'It's not important enough to be tragic, but it's a bit too sad to be comic.'

Journal IV

January

Afternoon. White light, hot dry wind blowing on the terrace. Stretched blue sky. Cool in the house.

A summer afternoon as in Brăila. Only I left to remember it.

Frank Auerbach, an exhibition of his work at Tate Britain, and Catherine Lampert's book about him: *Speaking and Painting*, reviewed by Mark Prince in the *Times Literary Supplement*.

'Born in Berlin in 1931 to Jewish parents and forced to emigrate to England, alone, at the age of seven, Frank Auerbach has always emphasised the positive results of his deracination. Describing the war years at Bunce Court, a genial boarding school in Kent, run by eccentric German refugees and British conscientious objectors, he told Catherine Lampert:

'We were enrolled as Wolf Cubs or Brownies, and did country dancing in the hall. And so, without any conscious effort we were anglicised.'

Any sense of loss lurking in the last sentence is thoroughly concealed. In *Frank Auerbach: Speaking and Painting*, we hear him talk of his background twice:

'I don't keep anything. It may be due to my background.

'I absolutely believe that you keep forging on, forwards, and that if you look back you turn into a pillar of salt.' And later:

'I was always aware of death because of my background. And in some curious way the practice of art and the awareness of the imminence of death are connected. Otherwise we would not find it necessary to do the work art finally does – to pin down something and take it out of time.'

Coming out of the Opera House with James, quite pleased with ourselves.

THE CITY, the city, a more marvellous spectacle than inside. The lights golden red, glowing, the night warm, and these mime artists on the steps, amazing black shapes with masks, other floating objects which they used to beautiful effect to form animals, boats, birds...

Odd shapes in the night in total silence.

An interview in the *Sydney Morning Herald* with Bob Gould of the famous Sydney Bookshop.

He hopes to live till eighty. He is seventy-four now. They were quoting him: 'I am hoping to last for a considerably longer period by the use of considerable ingenuity.'

I was hoping that we could use our ingenuity to that effect too, but unfortunately it did not work for him either.

He did not reach eighty.

February

Robert Hughes on Frank Auerbach:

'This ability to transform without romanticising is, among other things, what "maturity" means to a painter.

'It reminds us that painting may still connect us to the whole body of the world, being more than just a conduit for debate about novelty, cultural signs, and stylistic relations; that the shallowness, the vacuous proliferation of footnotes, to which the tyranny of art history has condemned it, in the name first of avant-gardism and then of post-modernism, can be revoked if the painter or sculptor is determined to play a deeper more direct game.

'What counts more...is the sense it projects of the immediacy of experience...in a way that is deeply meditated...Like all paintings good or bad, it is coded...But the clear purpose of its codes is to clarify Auerbach's struggle, not to "express himself" but to stabilise and define the terms of his relation to the real, resistant and experienced world; which is what art must do, today or yesterday, if it is to be more than chatter.'

Watching a film on the development of film. Humans have always tried to breathe life into dead matter.

March

Cooked all day for the dinner tonight. Very hot, as if the height of summer, a desert wind blowing, drying the washing.

The neighbour next door forever mixing concrete to build his dream house.

At one point she quoted someone saying that language is neutral. But languages are not neutral at all, on the contrary – CHARGED – with history, geography, power arrangements, changes that are absorbed continuously...

Evenings alone in the kitchen.

Only the sound of the perfectly white door, the shell-pink walls and the warm colour of the wooden floor.

The night empty but for the wind.

Black clouds over the city, the bridge...

Reading about Léon-Paul Fargue, 1876–1947.

Known mainly for *Le Piéton de Paris* about the city of Paris.

'As he scrutinizes the urban and social surfaces of the town, his writing never forgets that in the depths of us all, there is something indomitable and desperate that nothing ever changes.'

An interview with Almodóvar, the Spanish filmmaker, in the *Good Weekend*, by Lyn Hirschberg.

Asked about his latest film, whether it was autobiographical, and he: 'Everything that is not autobiographical, is plagiarism.'

And later discussing his love of glass: 'Glass is very optimistic. It holds possibilities in its beauty, a kind of hopefulness that is as fragile as glass.'

I think of glass as transcendental material. I imagine that Paradise would be full of glass...the transparency, the core of its luminescence, the balance it seems to have when the object is well made.

Easter at Victoria's. Beautiful warm day. Children in the pool, the water electric blue.

Someone asking if I am Jurgis' sister, and Jurgis quick as a flash:

'No, a cousin from Persepolis.'

We all laughed.

April

Discussions about travelling – Uluru – Leslie talking of her experience at the Centre, Uluru at dawn, the sun behind it, the rock looking like a magnificent spaceship.

Then the sun rising, the rocks changing colour with enormous rapidity, she was overwhelmed by the sight.

The desert, what an amazing place. The Olgas, some power in the landscape that goes beyond one's understanding. I said: 'Why do you think the Aboriginal people gave it such importance... we are dealing with powerful forces...hopefully we will come slowly to understand more about them...'

Michael Ondaatje and *Running in the Family*, what a sad, tragic book. The sequences of the monsoon, the rain, very alive...the animals in the forest, the death of the grandmother in the floods.

But all that drinking, his father, a kind of madness induced by alcohol, and his mother bringing up four children, and his father, in spite of his love for her... going on drinking, destroying himself...

What a sad end to all these lives, as if they could not come to terms with their idea of themselves in that environment, in that life.

Mother in the dream last night, as a presence in the kitchen, talking to me, only the impression of her care, her voice floating in the air. We were both peering into the dish to see if it is ready, an ongoing conversation.

Looking at books about Satie. On the last page of his biography – a photo of Satie with his hat on, his umbrella, and below it a caption in French:

Si je suis francais? Bien sur – pourquoi voulez-vous qu'un homme de mon age ne sois pas francais? Vous me suprenez...

Maybe I should start saying something similar when they ask me if I am Australian...

Am I an Australian? But of course, why do you think that a woman of my age is not Australian. You surprise me...

Satie – he is very good, sensitive, tragic, witty...

A series of retrospective films, the one last night made in the sixties, probably. An exhibition by Nolan about Ern Malley.

Max Harris, a young Dunstan, Dutton and so on.

A sort of naive and rather rough film in technical terms. Nolan speaking of the beautiful, subtle colours of Australia, as if rediscovering them.

But the types interviewed at the exhibition quite different from how Australians look today – men with mutton-chops, red hair, a more naive roughness than now.

Not many women in the film, even Cynthia, a glimpse of her by the sea, for the rest – men exhibiting, men interviewed, women shown only as 'good-looking sheilas' in the streets of Adelaide.

May

A program about five conductors and Mahler.

Riccardo Muti:

'The notes are there and his directions, but behind them the infinite possibilities.'

In the article they were tracing the history of epigrams.

The first Greek anthology in 900, compiled in Constantinople, by a Constantine Kefalas, they spelt it Cephalas.

The first time I have seen the name mentioned.

Fellini's film – *And the Ship Sails On* – some friends did not like it, this magical, inventive, ironic, light, beautiful work, poking fun at the musicians, their inflated ideas of themselves...and suddenly, in the most ridiculous situations producing this marvellous, moving music...

I loved it, totally elated by it, the subtlety of his approach, as if a beautiful piece of glass that is kept afloat by magical means.

A lot of movement in the dream last night. At a small table I was talking to Ritsos. He was tall, as in the photos, showing me some poems, a small notebook.

There were other people around, then he said that he could hear bells. I couldn't, he got up from the table and went out in the street, he said to me:

'I am quite religious, you know...'

I have been translating his last poems – *Seconds* – glimpses of brief moments with a wistful tone to them...

Last night I was watching this amazing film called *Oh My God* by Peter Rodger, interviewing the world, so to speak, about their definitions of God.

Beautifully photographed, every religion and place of worship. Only the Buddhists were missing.

I remember reading once a Buddhist monk's definition of God: 'Great emptiness and nothing holy in it.'

I was quite surprised.

But what the film proved, above all possible definitions was the human need for religion, for something external to themselves with some powers and an ethical direction and the necessity to connect with it.

Evening in the kitchen. Potatoes in the oven and Marinella singing.

Raining, wet and dark outside, only the traffic on the bridge, a distant series of moving lights.

An announcement of a new production of Molière's *The Miser*.

I remembered Rex Cramphorn's production of the *Imaginary Invalid*, a marvellous, fast-paced, witty performance, always in keeping with Molière, the period, the irony of the piece, the musical score well balanced, the right pathos in the position of the lovers, the love between them actually coming alive, always a difficult thing to achieve.

It put me in a marvellous mood at what the human spirit can achieve – the text sustained in its marvellous complexity, the best Molière I had seen.

By comparison, the mothballs production I saw later in Paris at the Comédie-Française, *The Miser*, nothing but an image of gloom, a diction in which language hardly made an impact.

They had gone for a historical reconstruction of the lighting at Molière's time, everything so dark that you could hardly see the faces of the actors, especially from where I was sitting.

June

The Sydney Film Festival in the State Theatre, our old friend. Lots of films in the magnificent building, opulent and elegant, full of mirrors, the sweeping, curved staircase, beautiful wood in warm colours.

This year, a retrospective of John Cassavetes, the Greek/ American director, a new discovery for me.

The wildness of life as an inner force, the camera tone at the beginning of *Minnie and Moskowitz*, the streets at night, the rubbish blown by the wind, the light from the restaurant on the pavements, you were immediately into life, immersed.

All these shifts of energy, negative, positive, men treating women as if they were objects at their disposal, the moment they were allowed to come near, the amazing rapidity with which even the most foolish of men presumes to be more knowledgeable, intelligent, etc....than women.

Then the scene of the two mothers, a marvellous piece, a model of wit.

I am telling everyone – we must see more Cassavetes...

In a program called *The Colour of Your Money* the selling of a Picasso at Sotheby's, the commentator:

'They are selling aesthetics now instead of morality or religion.'

Twenty-three million, a small painting, *At the Lapin Agile*, everything so unreal, so sinister.

Akhmatova last night, a film commemorating one hundred years since her birth.

Young students reciting her poems in elegant surroundings... What always moved me was that when she was asked to speak over the radio to the women of Leningrad – during the siege – she spoke of the Russian language, how we must save it, preserve it, pass it on to our children...language was the essential core of the country and the struggle...

Margaret came yesterday afternoon for a visit, and to tell me how much she liked *Alexia*, which she has just discovered. Music and the instruments, but the whole thing rather sad.

I asked about her writing. She is trying to write a book about her mother, finds it difficult. She did not like her, neurotic, cruel, writing about her before she always romanticised her, was feeling guilty about her feelings. Writing about her, she said, does not liberate you or solve the issue.

Not at all, I agreed. A dangerous activity as well, bringing things into the sharp focus required to write about them, they prove explosive in inner terms...and they remain much more defined so that you can have better access to them...

A very delicate face, warm brown hair. She was asking me if I have an agent. I laughed.

'Who will take me on,' I said, 'they will die of hunger with my type of writing.'

And she: I must not laugh about my work. 'I don't,' I said, 'I am laughing about market conditions.'

When we came out of the gallery it was very cold, the wind was blowing. We went to Chinatown via a long route, they had closed down some streets.

We had soup, blew our noses, laughed, the place as full of debris as before, we all looked rather unkempt, at that hour, before closing time.

At the Film Festival, the Mongolian grandmother commenting on a game of soccer:

'Twenty men running after a ball in their underpants. A game for morons.' Another view of the game.

As I came out after the downpour, the city full of wet, shiny streets, the red lights of the cars, the night quite fine now. Before, the scene would have seemed lyrical, but now a cooler eye.

July

With Mavis to Gleebooks to buy texts for her course.

I bought a book of interviews with Xenakis by Bálint András Varga.

Xenakis and Brăila, he was born in the city too, seemed to have spent the same time there as me.

Going to Brăila for his summer holiday in 1938, walking on the sand on the beach on the other side of the Danube and the city, where I was with Father, later, and thought that he had drowned, that day full of light and emptiness.

There, Xenakis discovered God for the first time.

Came home and announced to the family that GOD exists.

He changed his mind later.

I found this moving, the connection to the old places.

Listening to the radio this afternoon I thought of the resonances that music used to produce in me when I was young. The resonances people produced in me too, so that I was somehow in a constant state of alert.

Everything has become more quiet now, less impact.

I am trying to keep away from it too, not enough energy, now.

On the ABC a piece by Ravel composed in honour of a friend who was killed in the First World War...the critics found the piece not sombre enough for the occasion, and Ravel: 'The dead are sad enough in their eternal silence...'

Anna came and brought me as usual, a lot of magazines.

In the *New York Review of Books*, an article about an exhibition in Germany of Daumier's prints, cartoons.

Dear, dear Daumier, at the university, when I was totally desperate with our problems, I would go to the library and take out the heavy, large, earlier volumes of his prints, cheer myself up with his wit, his irony – his lawyers, politicians.

To the dentist waiting my turn, reading *Vogue*, an article about Robert Hughes, the art critic, in which he was saying that our first impulses towards art are always stimulated by bad art.

Then about a man called Lancaster with whom he did a program for the BBC, who was telling him that the amount of fornication going on in a society is stable at all times, only the extent to which it is talked about varies from century to century. He called this – the Lancaster Law.

Looking at old manuscripts trying to get rid of them, I feel somehow incapable as if I am destroying the past, the repetitive difficult work to try and express something, find the right language for it.

But the actual pieces of paper, the colour, the texture of the paper used, an immediacy about them, like an organism.

August

Bernard Smith being interviewed about his new book.

'From my lifelong experience of culture in this country, what I have to say in the book will not be taken seriously by Australians unless it is taken seriously in the Northern Hemisphere.

'It is not so much a matter of "cultural cringe", as of a geographical fact. The southern hemisphere consists mostly of SALT WATER.'

Reading interviews in the *Paris Review*, the mystery of writing remains untouched somehow – we learn about pens, notebooks, childhoods, life, experiences, characters one meets and so on...

But the actual transformation of this material into writing, writing of a certain kind, remains as mysterious as before...

The white cockatoo came back yesterday, walking awkwardly on the path, drinking water, hanging on to thin branches that do not sustain its weight...watching the ground carefully, the light flickering through the branches, all the other birds watching him, pecking the ground in a more careful way.

Black Sun – a beautiful, disturbing film by Gary Tarn, based on a bestselling autobiographical book by a painter and filmmaker – Hugues de Montalembert – who became blind after interrupting thieves in his apartment in New York, they threw paint thinner in his face...

A beautifully constructed film, his voice, the only narration, tracing his life after going blind.

His matter-of-fact descriptions of his own condition somehow trapped you in the condition itself. The images totally matched the narrative, even when they appeared disconnected.

They took you in, kept you there the whole time. Even though there was no action.

On TV a lot of discussions about disability.

A Commission will look at the issues. Is old age a disability?

Remembered Mrs C. Still at home at the time. A neighbour came to tell me that she wanted to see me.

A tall, heavy woman was there in Celia's absence.

Mrs C in her nightgown having tea, without her two front teeth, she still could not find them, complaining about the woman, describing her as 'an ogre', we laughed.

Mrs C:

'She is probably behind the door listening to us, she will come with a bucket of water to wash me...treats me as if I am a baby, my legs up...

'How are we going to solve this?' she asks.

A difficult question. But she seems okay, complaining about the woman who chopped her hair...

The big, solid woman is in the kitchen, tells me that Mrs C is gaga. I must not listen to her, she doesn't know what is going on.

I said: 'Treat her gently,' and she: 'I always treat her gently.'

But it is obvious that we are dealing with an institutional mind, army practices...

Maybe they should look for more imaginative people as well.

The Macquarie Pen Anthology is out, a lot of us not included. Elizabeth rings:

'Are you in it?'

'No, I don't think so. They have not asked for permission.'

They should have waited for her to die and then take her out, she has been in every anthology published so far.

She went to have a look at her books and found them good...all this in a comic tone...we were laughing on the phone.

Then, the following Wednesday, I bought the *Australian Literary Review* with Ivor's article.

He is very upset about it too, about all the omissions, angry that some of us have been totally effaced.

In the article he is trying to give a balanced view of the

situation, seeing that some of the editors are part of his department at the University of Western Sydney.

I rang Elizabeth to tell her to go and buy it. Elizabeth rings the next day:

'Yes, yes, he is negative about it, but NOT NEGATIVE ENOUGH.'

September

Vrasidas describing a poet as 'a talent-free zone'.

Oscar Wilde:

'A little sincerity is a dangerous thing and a great deal of it is fatal.

'All great ideas are dangerous.

'Nowadays the people know the price of everything and the value of nothing.

'To define is to limit.'

Wilde has remained alive, and his views are not only applicable now, but remain true.

'Nothing changes,' Kafka remarked with melancholy humour of his first book, a slim volume titled – *Meditation* –

'Eleven books were sold at Andre's store. I bought ten of them myself...I would like to know who has the eleventh.'

It is as if one is waiting for this living to happen to discover inwardly one's writing.

Such a slow development coloured by events, experiences...

On Saturday afternoon I watched a documentary called – *Pericles In America* – a klarino player from Epiros – Pericles Halkias.

A large group of people dancing at the edge of town to these amazing virtuoso sounds of a sad song:

Tell us Death
how is life
down there
in the darkness...

Pericles describing his life – a poor child with nothing to eat, no clothes, he began to play at dances when he was ten.

They said: 'This boy can play.'

So then he went on playing, later in Athens, a tour of America with Gounaris. In New York he went to play at the Istanbul Club, full of good musicians. They said to him: 'You should stay here.' So he stayed.

Everything okay, money and so on. His son plays the clarinet too, very well.

How much music has changed, all these commercial things in it, no purity of form, totally changed from what it was, clubs, amplification, a new generation with no knowledge of the past, everything mixed up – styles, forms, no line...

'That's what it is, all useless...'

'That's the adventure of my life.'

His conclusion.

October

Picasso:

'Painting is a blind man's profession. He paints not what he sees, but what he feels, what he tells himself about what he sees.'

Saul Bellow:
'The great weight of the unspoken left them little to talk about.'

Les Troyens by Berlioz at the Paris Opera directed and designed by Yannis Kokkos.

Cassandre, sung by an Italian soprano – Antonucci, very moving, unfolding like a Greek tragedy. The voices very good, the movements of the massive choir, a large, transparent backdrop that reflected the movements on stage, the outlines of Troy.

Everyone in dark clothes. Cassandre the only one in white, Antonucci looking very much like Irene Papas.

Most impressive. Norrington conducting.

Berlioz would have been pleased. To think how much he wanted to see the whole opera. Performed only in parts during his lifetime.

And his father who never heard any of his compositions played by an orchestra.

On the radio yesterday afternoon, *Capriccio Italien* by Tchaikovsky – the *marche funèbre* they used to play in Brăila during the funerals.

I immediately see the wide boulevard coming down from St Nikola, with the hearse and the black hooded plumed horses, and a sort of lament in the air, as one watched the procession and heard the brass band bellowing out these long, mournful sounds.

I met him down George Street. I had not seen him for a long time. Still busy with music, musicians, friendly, with his curly hair.

I still remember, the night at the Music Centre, under the bridge, his friends had come too, studious types, listening very seriously.

Through the large windows the sky like a blue, dark jewel, the moon rising over the sea, large and yellow, a hazy, mustard yellow, and below it, the ferries came and went cutting the water, as the sky grew darker and the moon rose up, paler and paler, more lights appeared, and inside he was nervously going through his paces.

He was talking about a magnificent sandouri player, the instrument with crisp sounds and lower, dark tones like a cello.

And the lutes...all these migrant musicians living in the suburbs, working in factories, this entire heritage not known to people, not touching anyone, surrounded by indifference.

Mavis waiting in Emergency after the terrible fall, marks on her face, and this man next to her:

'You poor bugger. You've been in a domestic.'

November

Notice at the Anglican Church in Broadway:

'Meet friends
Meet Jesus
Sunday at 4.30'

One hopes that he is keeping his appointment.

Going to town in the bus, at my back, this man with a booming voice, on his mobile, giving advice about shares, on and on, how to buy them, how to sell them, how to talk about them.

In front of me a young girl who came at the stop of the new flats. Expensive cotton blouse with pink cuff links, and a wristwatch that could direct an empire – large and gleaming black.

Dream.

I was in a public place sitting on a bench. Next to me the well-known writer was sitting dressed in red. She was questioning me about my arrival in Australia. How did I come, did I miss Europe and so on. Her tone slightly aggressive.

I was responding in a neutral tone.

Then she said:

'Did you think that Australia would adjust to you?'

'No,' I said, 'I was hoping that we would adjust to each other.'

I got up. I was walking around. But she went on pestering me with her questions. I was answering superficially, while conducting some inner monologue with myself, counteracting all her questions in silence.

Then I woke up.

Yesterday afternoon with Yota to hear a talk by Panaiota about Margarita Karapanou.

I had begun to read her book, *Kassandra and the Wolf*, a savage sort of writing that reminded me of Sylvia Plath's last poems, surreal, but brutal.

A sort of savagery of fairy tales. We watched an interview she gave two years before she died. Breakdowns, breakdowns...in bed for a whole year, hospitals like places of torture, where the doctors were on one side and the patients on the other...electric shocks...

She came from an old Athenian family, her mother, a writer too, living in Paris, the daughter moved between Athens and Paris.

Disturbing stuff, very close to the bone. One needs a lot of courage to take it in.

December

Suddenly a wave of warm weather, the new green leaves of the apricot tree transparent in the light, the music on the radio full of possibilities, the horizon, the light on the terrace.

Looking at old photos, our journeys north, and my line that I wanted to use in some short story:

'A dispirited fox was crossing the road at Fowler's Gap.'

I was telling Nadine about it, she liked foxes too.

How she stops at night when coming from a concert, in Lane Cove Park, she stays for a while in the dark. The park teaming with wildlife.

One night, a fox came out and stood there watching her, she wanted to come out and stroke her…

This golden eagle that was living on the roof of her house by the sea, its pantaloons blowing in the wind, a beautiful creature with amazing eyesight, he would dive down the rocks four hundred feet below and pick up a water rat…

An *Apache* in George Street –

Short white hair, number one cut. Dark blue trousers, and red jacket, red shirt, blue tie with red hearts on it.

His body posture as if coming from Platia Avissinias in Athens.

He was watching the bus with a slightly choleric expression on his face.

Then he took out a packet of cigarettes, produced from his pocket a ten-centimetre-long cigarette holder, carved wood with a heavily sculpted surface.

We left him there, past Gowings, heavy silver rings, knuckle dusters…

We saw again Renoir's *The River*, yesterday afternoon. It has remained a beautiful, moving, lyrical film, human and immediate…keeping its balance of sentiment and experience very well, especially in such a difficult age as adolescence.

Later I looked at Bazin's book on Renoir, the entire approach to criticism quite different, a language that involved immediate responses, art in itself, lines of analysis and so on.

An enthusiasm for the medium that differs totally from today's critical writing…something clinical, tight and not at ease today… all those mean theoretical views that have been prevailing…

Mavis – encounter with this widower from Singleton describing things in the country:

'So dry, you could flog a flea in the paddock.'

Conversations With Nadia Boulanger by Bruno Monsaingeon –

The famous music teacher, subtle, full of good will towards music, the students, the talent of the young – Lipatti, Markevitch, relationships with a lot of the musicians of her day – Enesco, Stravinsky, Copland, Bernstein, Virgil Thomson, Elliott Carter.

Nadia Boulanger on her teaching:

'I had to insist on a knowledge of essentials. In other words, how to listen, look, hear and see. And then, on having the kind of self-respect which is not assertive, but does attach importance to being. And I believe that if you do not value existence, you cannot play well, you can not think well, you can not live well.

'I believe that a work of art transcends all its interpreters.'

Lolo sent me *Murasaki Shikibu: Her Diary and Poetic Memoirs* – eleventh century, the author of *The Tale of Genji*.

Lovely, at ease, intelligent writing, as if reading a friend who tells you of the happenings at the Emperor's court.

Descriptions of courtiers, ladies at the court, marvellously dressed, as well as remarks about the scene, ironies...

The impact of beautiful clothing, materials, combination of colours, the whole scene alive with personalities, protocol, power.

Some of her poems translated by Richard Bowring:

Birds on the water:
Can I look at them

Dispassionately?
I too am floating through
A sad uncertain world.

Be close, you say:
But the first thing I met
On getting close
Were your feelings,
Thin as summer clothes.

For how long
Should we long for those
Already gone?
Today's grief
Is our own tomorrow.

Journal V

January

Heat and silence, the light only falling on the plants, the terrace.

Terribly sad suddenly in the afternoon, in the silent house with the brilliant light outside, thinking of all the people that have gone.

I had dreamt of Father, he was wiping his eyes in the well-known gesture and telling me that he is not feeling well.

'But what is it?' I asked.

Some vague reply that I don't remember.

When I open the drawers I see the tapes that he made playing the violin, but don't have the courage to listen to them. I imagine that *The Legend* by Wieniawski would be there.

Dream.

Agitated night. Running somewhere. But towards morning dreamt that I was looking at this large, empty room, parquet floor, totally empty walls.

A woman was there sitting on the floor unravelling a ball of wool, helped by a tall, impeccably dressed man, in grey trousers, vest, tie, very upright, moving about the room, helping her place the wool on the floor, but the man had no head, just a square shape coming out of his neck, yet he moved well, as if he could see.

I was an outsider, watching, totally horrified at the headless man, the neck metallic, silver-grey. Some sort of creation of cinematic machinery, but he seemed totally alive and moving with purpose.

A sort of de Chirico set up...empty rooms, wooden floors and impeccably dressed men without heads...

Watching again the Le Clézio interview, the Nobel Prize winner, he seemed to be very aware of being a member of an elite group, he felt that writers are part of an elite group and not part of ordinary life.

He is looking at ordinary life, wants to write about it. I don't feel that I am part of an elite group or that I am looking at ordinary life from outside, I am in it, trying to express it by some direct means.

He is searching for his childhood self, he feels that the early impressions are what one writes about.

But I don't feel that, life, a continuous process, one moves with it, changes with it.

Just finished a biography of Foucault...events, according to the book, affect concepts not men...what does that mean?

He went to Iran before the Revolution, later he met the Ayatollah, history in the making, but events always surpass our imagination.

He somehow did not catch a whiff of the new fanatics.

He hated the Shah, was angry with an Iranian woman who wrote about what was coming.

February

Maybe I am not in touch with the current visual arts directions – cannot find an access into the whole thing. All these archival documents, factualities, sounds of the street, cut up words, piles of arranged discarded objects and so on...they don't seem to engage me, material to me undigested, that does not bear the marks of a sensitivity that has absorbed them, made them part of itself, brought them out in some meaningful form.

On the walls of galleries long intellectual explanations of what the work is about.

In the last issue of the *Times Literary Supplement* an article about the translation prizes, quoting some of the extravagant language, as English speakers would see it, of Spanish, Portuguese and other foreign writers.

António Lobo Antunes – *The Land at the End of the World*, a novel set in Angola:

'On the second day we reached Madeira, a fruitcake decorated with crystalized houses floating on the blue china tray of the sea.'

Or the Swedish poet Harry Martinson:

Then I remembered bygone years
An evening with Desdie
Stars shone cleanly
She slipped along the path and met me
and my heart thumped
and the bats swooped on Louisiana.

Liked them all, very alive.

Thinking of the talk...she went on saying about the failure of Australian society to look at itself, to come to grips with what is happening, with the transformations, to allow these transformations to be expressed as a natural part of our imaginative environment.

Instead, everyone is cramped intellectually, socially and imaginatively by theories and approaches which have long been dead, and which allow for no growth.

Again a constant desire to remain at an imitation level, an imitation of England, of America, as if what was here must of necessity be second rate, as if we could not find our own means of assessing imaginatively our positions, our relationship to this landscape in whatever way we can, and the more different the approaches the better, hoping that out of this amalgam of views some of the intrinsic directions will become evident in time.

Seeing Mavis after the operation in hospital –

Mavis, as if blown by a savage wind.

An article by John Lanchester with the title 'Pursuing Happiness':

Two scholars explore the fragility of contentment, review the history of the concept from earlier times to now...their final definition:

'...the state of immersion in a task that is challenging yet closely matched to one's abilities ...'

March

Reading Yoshida Kenkō, a Japanese poet of the fourteenth century, his book called – *Essays in Idleness* – described as a miscellany of aphorisms, musings and anecdotes. Some of his thoughts:

Disagreeable things are:
Too much furniture in a living room.
Too many pens in an inkstand.
Too many images in a private shrine.
Too many rocks, herbs, and trees in a garden.
Too many children in a house.
Too many words when men meet.
Too many vows in a prayer.

Things of which it is good to see plenty:
Books in a bookcase.
Dust in a dust heap.

And later:

There was a certain man, a sort of local sheriff, in Tsukushi, who held that the radish was a cure for all evils, and every morning, for years, he ate two of them cooked.

One day, taking advantage of the absence of people from his residence, the enemy fell upon him, attacking from all sides. When suddenly, two warriors appeared in the house, and fighting without any regard for their lives, drove them all back.

Greatly mystified, he asked who they were that had been so good as to fight on his behalf.

Whereupon they said:

'We are the radishes which you have trusted and eaten every morning for years,' and vanished.

Such virtue was there in his great faith.

George's new book:

George Michelakakis

Hope in Crisis: Culture and Art in a time of Globalization

Design and cover by Frixos Ioannidis

A large, impressive book on Greek/Australian artists covering both poetry and the visual arts.

Scholarly, wide-ranging, it includes not only the first generation but the second generation born in Australia. Beautiful reproductions of paintings, photos.

Using Greek mainly in the text, but quoting works in English as well.

A first, in terms of such analysis and inclusions. George worked on it for eight years.

Let us hope for some readers.

Watching the concert in Vienna...all these singers...Lucia Popp, very good and others...full of loveliness...The singing, watching a body sing, the absorption into this magnificent power, this breath that rises from inside, that is constantly controlled to produce these delicate, or powerful sounds, this torch, flame of vibration, this total inner concentration...

April

Late afternoon, a cold wind had come up. I was in the kitchen looking at the whitish light, the empty day, all this death and heroism on the radio, on television.

Elderly men and women with white hair marching, the priests

talking of patriotism, politicians...

And the dead, underground, as usual, what were they saying? Should countries always define themselves by war?

Last night dreamt of H. He was in a place that looked like a cemetery, but not the one at Botany. Bushes with flowers, pink, the overall effect. On the ground a large, oblong shape, like a coffin, a cello. He was sitting on it, he seemed very small and he was smoking.

I asked him: 'Why are you sitting there?'

And he: 'The grave is empty.'

He seemed peaceful and rather resigned.

Thinking of him. He led a life of resistance, they could never make him sociable, integrated, he led his life in silence, indifferent to a certain extent, ironic, resisting all the extreme measures of such institutions.

Taking his walks in the rain, in that green country, smoking his cigarettes, and thinking his own unconfessed thoughts.

Only from time to time he would come out with some little philosophical remark: '...Everything is ephemeral...'

Thursday night at Sydney University to hear Vrasidas talking about Aristotle. A lively talk, interesting to hear about the background of his life. At the court of the Macedonian King, tutor to Alexander, he came to Athens, the Athenians did not like him, were suspicious of him – he, associated with demagogues.

He was working with students, searching, but in spite of his attention to structures, details and so on, he too was looking down on women, apparently he thought that they had fewer teeth than men, a mark of their inferiority.

After he died, his works unknown for two centuries, then rediscovered.

Lela rang in the afternoon crying...we lost Giulia...

Giulia, the tall, handsome girl with milky white face, and the green eyes, statuesque.

Falling in love with this young man from the next little town, tall like her and good-looking too, following her everywhere, even though his parents were against her, finally getting married.

We went to visit her in her new home – the village, the orchards...We went into the little cottage, two rooms of solid stone, woven rugs hanging, pieces of embroidery, somehow an environment created by someone else in which she was trying to fit her city life, not managing very well.

She seemed to have lost her courage already, and looked like a prisoner, between the husband that had transformed from the dashing young man, into something of a bully, the child that was lying in an elaborate wooden cot, that had been in the family for generations.

We went for lunch after we were shown the almond plantation by the husband.

The lunch in the big house.

We all sat at the long, heavy wooden table, carved and solid, dark earthenware pots with the food.

The in-laws were sitting, sour-looking and silent, disapproving of the marriage, this useless city girl that could not work in the fields and had to be kept by them.

A darkness inside them that would require some archaic language to be able to express it...a language of strong herbs boiled at full moon.

Reading Henry James on his friendship with Conrad – uneasy – but he liked his writing. He wrote to the Royal Literary Fund in 1904, this very nice letter about the difficulties of someone writing in a new language, in support of an application by Conrad for some financial help.

Conrad – later of James:

'I admired him very much, he accepted my admiration as a gift worth having.'

May

In the plane travelling to Melbourne, thinking of writers, writing, critics. An arid period for writers, at least for writers like myself.

The kid next to me talking to his father:

'I am listening to the ocean, Dad.' Holding the shell to his ear.

'How come you can hear the ocean, Dad?'

The mysteries of the world.

A review by William Armstrong of a new book about Nazim Hikmet, called – *The Assassin from the Apricot City* – by Witold Szablowski.

'Turkey's greatest twentieth-century poet – Nazim Hikmet – was a third-generation immigrant of aristocratic Polish stock...'

This is what I like about origins, their unpredictability.

Hikmet defines poets as: 'The tongue of the unseen...'

Randall Jarrell in the *New York Review of Books*, on Ezra Pound:

'He has taken all cultures for his province, and is naturally a little provincial about it.'

Yesterday in town to meet Sarah and get the printed letterheads. Very hot, a hot wind blowing as if early spring.

Sarah's work as usual, nice, clean, elegant lines.

Inside the building, the Lending Library of Fiction, Romance, Detective stories...the oldest in Australia.

Sarah among this group of women, all volunteers, she the Secretary of the Library.

They were all making sandwiches, serving them, making some money for the club.

An old-fashioned atmosphere of Britishness, egg-curry sandwiches, salmon with shredded lettuce, the only change, the bread – brown bread.

Soups, as well as tea, and tall, thin men in windcheaters, and rather large women in cardigans and skirts, but quite nice. We spoke with Sarah while she was making the sandwiches, I serving them.

Came home carrying the printed letterheads.

Suddenly winter, fallen leaves on the ground, the wind cold, and the heaters in the house.

Began reading Hannah Arendt, very good, reviews and essays, an interesting complex voice. I rather liked her.

I sometimes feel that the fear of this end towards which we are imperceptibly going is so terrifying that people do anything in order to forget – start wars, are full of hatred, kill, build enormous empty structures which they have to sustain by an enormous amount of energy.

Stendhal in his life of Rossini, describing the field of opera commissions in Italy at the time, and then: '...there is no intolerance like that of a man of artistic sensibility...'

June

Mark Strand, the American poet, has died. I always thought of him, as I saw him briefly in Sydney, a long time ago, tall, with a very strong face, the type of face one imagines when young and reading romantic novels, that the hero would have. High cheek bones, a soft voice, lumbering sort of gait, very human eyes.

His wife was studying Greek, remarks on my name, a restrained but warm quality about her.

They both seemed to be at ease with us.

And then, that moving poem I have been reading from time to time:

'Black Sea'
One clear night while the others slept, I climbed
the stairs to the roof of the house and under a sky
strewn with stars I gazed at the sea, at the spread of it,
the rolling crests of it raked by the wind, becoming
like bits of lace tossed in the air. I stood in the long,

whispering night, waiting for something, a sign, the approach
of a distant light, and I imagined you coming closer,
the dark waves of your hair mingling with the sea,
and the dark became desire, and desire the arriving light.
The nearness, the momentary warmth of you as I stood
on that lonely height watching the slow swells of the sea
break on the shore and turn briefly into glass and disappear…
Why did I believe you would come out of nowhere? Why with all
that the world offers would you come only because I was here?

From an interview he gave to the *Paris Review*:

'I don't think it's human, you know, to be that competent at life.'

Watching a program on Nijinsky's *L'après-midi d'un faune* by Debussy.

Remember H, he always spoke about it. I wonder what significance it had for him in Bucharest? A significance one did not know at the time, nor later. All this illusion of understanding constantly pursuing us, later, much later, when people have gone, as with Mother, one realises the false nature of one's understanding, the moment viewed from a different point of view, with hardly any knowledge at all of what made it.

As with relationships, between Mother and Father, all those undercurrents that one guessed sometimes but never knew what they signified.

The Cavafy Academic Symposium.

Poor Cavafy, totally cut up, cooked with the new theories,

theories he knew nothing of, aspects even of gayness that he might not have approved of.

Made into a strange personality, his voice altered through so many intellects.

The women academics – softer voices and more relative, the men, more obsessive, attacking.

July

In the *Herald* an obituary on the death of the Earl of Harewood, the interesting, intelligent music-lover, working in the arts, a friend of Callas…

He was one of the few royals who genuinely valued British music. The obituary was quoting the Queen:

'As the Queen herself once put it to the general director Peter Jonas, on a rare visit to the English National Opera: "Funny thing about George. You know, in most respects he's perfectly normal."'

Rostropovich conducting Shostakovich's 11th Symphony.

Very arresting, dark, ominous inner landscapes, powerful, amazing changes of tone.

The Russians, one forgets their passionate power…

Alexis Wright won the Miles Franklin Award, interviewed on television, constantly referred to as an Aboriginal writer, we don't seem to have Irish writers…etc…

A lived face, resigned, telling us her complaints about the

whites. She feels the Aboriginals are doing their best to close the gap, but the other side is not interested.

Her grandmother was taken as a little girl, together with another little girl, by a white man, a pastoralist.

What happened to their families? The children don't know. A massacre probably, unmentioned.

The first writer for a long time to speak of deeper things, myths, cultural understandings, maybe some rapprochement can happen between the cultures, myths and the Aboriginal person.

I liked her, a real person, a sort of mild explosiveness in her manners, not giving in.

Chamfort:

'Nature never urges me – Be not poor, much less, be rich; she shouts: Be independent.'

August

Past twelve o'clock. Looking at the city from the upstairs window. The moon rising above the houses, on the right, next to the red tower, hanging silently above the city. Like half a slice of orange, sharply cut.

Elizabeth rings this morning. The Japanese family that lived on the same floor has now returned to Japan. The little boy is writing her an aerogram about his activities.

He went to the zoo, the animals he saw there, a long list – including emus, horses. Then he went to a fair, spring festivals in

Japan, and after describing some more adventures he ends with: 'My tooth fell off.'

His name – Rensuki – but if you are intimate with him you can call him Ren.

We laughed. I said to Elizabeth – we must ring the ABC and give them some alternative news to all the dreadful things that are happening around the world.

Watching Bergman's *The Seventh Seal* – still very good, alive, terrible. Death looking a very reasonable, indifferent personage, softly spoken.

Fear. Fear above all things, and the church, a terrible institution.

No one produces films like this any more, metaphysical concerns are totally out.

The black-and-white very good, luminous.

The knight and his companions returning home after ten years of fighting in the Crusades. The same zeal as now, zeal for war, no one is looking for alternative methods that can resolve things without killings, making for more human solutions that can prove real and less disruptive to life.

Weapons – their first idea...

Anna in hospital after the knee operation describing the voice of the physiotherapist:

'A voice that can cut through concrete.'

Back from Canberra. The weather crisp and sunny. Canberra an empty place, with no life somehow, only well-kept parks, lots of trees and clinical-looking buildings.

Dinner as usual at the Greek Club photographing ourselves with the replicas of the famous Greek statues, Poseidon, from the Archaeological Museum in Athens. Replicas that have become green-grey with time.

Later in the car talking of travels, Jolanta trying to convince Paul that going to Broken Hill and the Menindee Lakes was an absolute necessity for him...

We laughed, the streets empty and the wattle trees in flower.

The Gathering –

Time had passed over our faces leaving a fine print.

Only the voices tried to maintain their former form against this buffeting, still some traces of the old, former elegance.

September

From time to time the ABC plays something by Peggy Glanville-Hicks, none of her major works. Only James fighting all his life to put on one of her operas, every year some glimmer of hope, and then everything collapsing.

Remembered her in Greece where he sent me to visit her. She was living in a lovely house below the Acropolis.

Remembered the evening in James's apartment, dinner, looking at old photos – the Blackmans, Barbara and Charles when young, both youthful and full of light...Nadine...

During the evening I kept watching, was drawn to this object on top of the bookcase, a marvellously shaped object, onyx-coloured, shiny, lean, as if pared down to an essential form that looked like a bull's head, the essential abstraction of a bull's head.

Before I left I asked James what it was, he took it down to reveal a Greek vase given to him by Peggy, an original fifth-century.

Touching it, it was of a delicacy of texture as if human, the black mixed with brown ochre, like hair, something that someone had breathed through.

Coming home Mother was watching a French documentary, an analysis of the dilemma of modern Greece, between a total humanism and a total nihilism, if it could hold to the vital centre between the two...they finished by quoting a line from Sophocles' *Antigone*: 'man goes through all to arrive at nothing...'

Language, I was thinking last night, a miracle of an equal if not surpassed kind to music. I thought again of all this potential, its possibilities, as if a vast palace with enormous space, colours, lines. This is after all the essence of every good writer, the re-shaping of all this potential, an incandescent life that re-discovers for the readers a new language, so that they feel they are in front of a miracle.

Borges speaking of his father, who said, in fact we do not remember the past, but we constantly remember the memory of one moment, and then the memory of the memory and so on, till there is nothing firsthand any longer, so to speak, but constantly re-making, re-making under different circumstances on the basis of that moment.

Yesterday listening to the radio, this song in Russian.

I thought it was Vishnevskaya, a voice with emotional implications, carrying some charge, while Western European voices are too clean somehow, linear, inwardly thin now.

As if the recording methods have taken away everything that the producers think that the public will not like.

Looking at the plants at the back, total silence after the high winds, the rain...like a passion that has been spent.

October

Angelopoulos's film *Voyage to Cythera* – such a terribly sad film, an awkward, dark, terrible sadness, with no beginning and no end.

Nothing in the long run to relieve it, the silence of the people who are not expressing themselves, but take everything in in silence.

All this minimal dialogue

'It is me.'

'Have you eaten?'

What lives. Why does a political idea always make people lay down their lives, while an ongoing humanistic approach bores everyone?

The returning father, husband, still sustained by the same type of set ideas, and still sure of their truth, sure of his opinions, of his judgement, aware mostly of his own needs, never putting himself in the position of his wife, the children.

As Mother used to say: 'Everyone with their truth.'

But such a fanatical use of your own truth?

Nikos sent a beautiful catalogue of his exhibition in Vienna. I remembered our beginnings, visiting him in Melbourne, and meeting Dimitri for the first time.

He insisted that I should read *Nadja* by Breton.

'A seminal book.'

A clever, intellectual tour de force, but the woman, no feeling or understanding of her, an object, a duplicity in his approach covered by intellectual pyrotechnics.

A method of showing his cleverness, his friends, the fantastic interrelations that happen in life, but Nadja, a condescension in his tone when speaking of her.

The state of love – a time of great vulnerability. As Camus said about – *La Princesse de Clèves*:

'L'amour met l'être en danger...'

Love places the self in danger...

Reading Vivienne's thesis on Hinduism, a hatred of women that becomes a terrible oppressiveness for women. They cannot do this or that, they always need the company of a man to guide them, and so on...

Polluted when menstruating, the elements that produce life considered polluting. Then they have to undergo purification, the child as well, when born.

Quite tiresome really.

The Egyptians last night on TV – the men always have the best seats in the universe, eternal, an entire game that provided them with the entry into the eternal…

Some quotes to bring us to reality:

Heraclitus: 'Treasure seekers dig much and find little.'

Edgar Alan Poe: 'This fever called living.'

Laughing with James about the fate of our books. I with *Alexia* and 1631 copies left unsold, he with Macmillan 1500 copies left. They offered them to him at 50 cents a copy, but in the meantime sent him an account that he owes them $700.

Voices seem to be the ones that remain truer to their essence.

James, a few weeks before he died, the same articulated voice, the implications of a complex vocabulary still standing. He was trying to convince the Ubud Festival to invite me…

Dear, dear James, these were his last words to me…

On SBS a program on the American Indians, very good.

'To breathe is to pray.'

How they were stopped from performing their rituals that kept the world going, by the Catholic Church, and had to go underground, performing them at night.

A new biography of T.S. Eliot by Lyndall Gordon.

One can understand him better, but still not like him.

All this quest for God, sainthood, the church, sin, guilt…

His belief somehow does not seem genuine to me, a public personality expressing opinions on everything –

religion, tradition, writing.

No affection for life – somehow, a thin, inner man.

Then this idea that he had of CONTAMINATION – life as a contamination. He wanted to be pure, to reach some miracle of transubstantiation – but all a forced business, not a direct faith that could carry him there.

We are going with Yota to the Alexander the Great Club in Marrickville to hear Vrasidas talk about Tsitsanis – the famous composer of Greek songs and a virtuoso bouzouki player.

From the outside the building looks like a factory.

In the entrance, a large glass cabinet with memorabilia of Alexander – photos, plaster heads, large coins, folk costumes.

We are meeting downstairs, in the restaurant, already a large audience seated, a stage in the middle full of amplifiers.

The walls covered with large, gaudy paintings of the Parthenon...Alexander on horseback crossing the Alps, an imitation of David.

Then Vrasidas arrives carrying his computer, but the place is not set up to show slides. It takes a long time for things to be stitched up.

But we forget all this with Tsitsanis, images of Trikala, his home town, rebetika players, dancers holding small tables with their teeth...We see Tsarouchis, the well-known painter, with white hair now dancing.

Everyone sings, knows the songs, a part of their lives, the usual audience, all of us elderly, the women heavy, the men bald, Vrasidas's students in front, young and lovely looking.

Then Odyssea, the Kenyan, gets up and sings...Cloudy Sunday...

Cloudy Sunday...Cloudy like my heart...

A very good documentary on the Spanish architect Calatrava – large buildings, railway stations, bridges, in Spain, Portugal, France.

Beautiful structures, organic, elegant, well resolved with simplicity, surprising one with this poetry in space.

He is using natural shapes – trees, waves, the movement of the body, the articulation.

He talked of forces he had to take into account, he is an engineer/architect.

Most of his structures seem to be white – a rail station, platforms supported by columns made in the shape of trees, a white forest, very light.

I was most impressed.

December

Dream.

I seemed to be in a place of transit, trying to get away. Halls that were full of people before, but now they were all empty, large, dark, with high ceilings.

Suddenly out of the darkness a cello began to play, a noble, beautiful sad music.

The beginnings of a concerto that I could not identify. It must have been H playing.

The sound of the cello out of that darkness, moving, as if coming out of the past.

Elizabeth disappointed with the reviews of the short stories, constantly referring to them as bleak and depressing.

I told her:

'You are an idealist disappointed with the imperfections of the world and some people.'

Thinking of what I shall say in the interview.

The question she is posing – a definition of an Australian-Greek aesthetic...

How can one define it? Is there such a beast? Who is aware of it? Are there enough works to create an aesthetic?

How is an aesthetic created? Mostly in retrospect, I feel.

What sort of analysis can we offer outside the fact that we write mostly about a non-Anglo-Saxon group, from attitudes that the locals would consider foreign, in an English that seems equally un-Australian...maybe too flamboyant...more concerned with an immediacy viewed differently from the local writers.

Can all of us put together constitute a group with some similar characteristics?

The only things we can pose are questions.

They were in her garden, under the white beach umbrella. One wondered what Mrs C would have thought of it.

Windy. The laughter of the women came in waves. They were barbecuing.

Mrs C would have been annoyed by their presence, the barbecue, lowering the tone of the neighbourhood.

Ten years since she has died and in the meantime, her place populated by a lot of strangers.

Christmas – the time of emptiness and expectations.

Watching Louise Bourgeois's DVD last night.

Very dark elements and slightly sinister. I liked her early work, more light in it, the forms lighter.

The spider, she said, 'her most successful form', the spider is her mother, a feminine noun in French.

Her face riveting, I assume in her nineties now, as if made of the bark of a small tree, a slender tree, full of serrations coming down from her forehead, as if made by liquid time...

A lot of energy to her, anxious, bursting out of every corner of her body...limbs, sex, children, fear, insomnia, a constant analysis of her family life, things from her childhood still discussed as current events.

Disputing the question of sculpture and materials, learning to use them and so on. 'Materials are materials.' The important issue is emotion, and the direction it pushes one.

Her mother – intelligent, working steadily, her father emotional – she inherited both.

Her two sons were there, tall and friendly looking.

Journal VI

January

An article about *The Age of Wonder*.

They were quoting Joseph Banks, his *Endeavour* journal. Travelling to these parts of the world.

'They had heard that we were great Philosophers, and expected much from us, one of the first questions that they asked was, when it would thunder.'

Nabokov's letters to his wife Vera, a few of them translated from the Russian by Olga Voronina, Brian Boyd and Dmitri Nabokov.

In 1942 unable to find a job, he had embarked on a two-month lecture tour of colleges in Atlanta, Minnesota and so on.

'I walked for an hour and went to bed around eight. On the way a lightning bolt of undefined inspiration ran right through me. A passionate desire to write, and to write in Russian. And yet, I can't.

'I don't think anyone who hasn't experienced this feeling can understand its torment, its tragedy.

'English, in this sense is an illusion, and an ersatz.

'In my usual condition i.e. busy with butterflies, translations, or academic writing, I myself don't fully register the whole grief and bitterness of the situation.

'Cotton Woolley hotel, rain outside the window, a Bible and a telephone book in my room, for the convenience of communication with Heavens and the Office...'

A programme on Fiona Hall, her commission for the Botanical Gardens...and she:

'...people are still incredibly seduced by plants...'

In the gallery we looked at McCahon, his religious paintings. Misia liked the early ones, the ones with the writing left her unmoved.

But the lightness, the finesse of the colours, the amazing resolution of the paintings, the Ten Stations of the Cross, the line of the hills that plunges through the darkness.

And later, the long canvases, walking by the sea in memory of his mother and J. K. Baxter, the poet, who died in 1972, the ethereal whiteness, golden brown tones, very subtle and luminous at the same time.

What I liked about it, as you moved along it, was the feeling that you were undertaking an inner journey.

Anna rang yesterday. Her visit to New Zealand was good. Meeting old friends, a landscape she likes, homely somehow.

She was watching children playing on the beach, one felt that time was still, and that the gestures were being repeated over generations.

Reading about Ionesco, he comes out very human. One of his sayings:

'God is dead. Marx is dead. And I don't feel so well myself.'

A haiku by Basho:
In my new robe
this morning –
someone else.

February

Listening to Auden reading his poetry, to Eliot and others, their voices now sounding somehow artificial.

Auden: 'The primary function of poetry, as of all the arts, is to make us aware of ourselves and the world around us.

'I do not know if such increased awareness makes us more moral or more efficient: I hope not. I think it makes us more human, and I am quite certain it makes us more difficult to deceive, which is why, perhaps, all totalitarian theories of state, from Plato downwards, have deeply mistrusted the arts. They notice and say too much, and the neighbours start talking...

'Art is not magic, i.e. a means by which the artists communicates or arouse their feelings in others, but a mirror in which they may become conscious of what their own feelings really are, its proper effect, in fact is disenchanting.'

A fine rain, humid, late afternoon yesterday it cleared totally, blue sky, a slight wind and at night this brilliant, totally full round moon in the sky.

Slowly it disappeared behind some clouds, apricot pink light, and then nothing, just this light that seemed to suffuse the clouds above the line of the horizon, slightly off the bridge...

In the morning on the radio, a César Franck sonata that Father used to play at home, with the wistful, haunting beginning.

Another death.

But life goes on relentlessly as if afraid, afraid itself of death.

Maybe God is afraid too of this disappearance, as if of necessity he needs us, a mirror in which his definition lies, otherwise how can one explain this relentless drive to live, to regenerate, propagate with such terrible tenacity.

Constant discussions about wars, big and small, unsolved most of them. I remember the beginning of the Iraq War.

I had gone shopping. At the grocers they kept telling me that the WAR had started.

When I came back I put the television on. The WAR had started.

All these amazing television performances, everyone in front of cameras, at ease, enormous confidence in the medium, the world at their fingertips. Large groups of correspondents, footage of the front, the bombings, interviews, politicians, White House spokesperson...

All the signs of a major power, with immense resources, they themselves carried forward by this image, the image had become the substance of the war, while we, and thousands of others were watching this performance, hooked on it, addicted to this image of omnipotence that they exuded, euphoria – everyone was in it. They had gone over the country, bombing strategic targets with the new weapons, all the boys were watching to see how they were performing, measuring themselves with the other side.

March

I waited in the queue to have his book signed.

'Keep on writing,' he said to me, 'if I can make it, you can make it.'

I went out of the bookshop and walked down Glebe Point Road. The street full of the scents of food being cooked – Asian cooking.

The night above the trees and the lighted shops, young people eating hamburgers at the edge of cars. At the bus stop, two young women elegantly dressed, were eating fish and chips sitting on the steps of the closed shop...and the bus was not coming.

Then suddenly, on the other side of the street he was walking with three members of his publishing house. They were taking him to water, you could see their faces in the windows, discussing, all about merchandise and selling, one assumed, other more mysterious ways of selling.

The writing, left out of the discussion, it was probably feeling lonely.

To the opera last night. *Onegin*, a cluttered, unintelligent production. Good voices, Nicole Carr impressive as Tatyana, Dalibor Jenis as Onegin, vocally okay, but unimpressive as a presence, not very convincing, looking more like a second-rate seducer, than an intellectual weary of life and people.

A co-production with the Royal Opera House, Covent Garden and Fondazione Regio, Turin, director Kasper Holten.

A didactic sort of solution to the opera, totally destroying the lyricism of the piece and having constantly the heroes' younger selves on stage, getting in everyone's way, as if we could not imagine the younger selves of the heroes without being given them in physical form.

One single set, rather artificial, fields that looked unreal and painted, a chorus of elderly men, hardly looking like peasants.

A confused production. After the duel, Lensky remains dead at the front of the stage till the end of the opera, lying on the floor, unhappy, I assume...

But the music very warm and full of the passion of youth. Konstantin Gorny as Prince Gremin was good, and that lovely aria about loving Tatyana.

Nicole Carr – a great find.

Watching Tarkovsky – *The Mirror* – these amazing juxtapositions of images, music that creates an atmosphere of dreams, of some other world...the individuals, the children caught in this terrible element of life at a time of war.

Houses, interiors, nature, the wind moving suddenly and in unexpected ways, as if a person.

But sad...very sad...full of silences...

April

Last night – *Foreign Correspondent* on the ABC – the Catholic Church and the non-payment of taxes.

Rome looking marvellous at night, during the day with the snow, the Italians looking good, articulate, the language itself always sounding very warm, musical.

Eric Campbell managed to speak to high Vatican officials, looking as they should, the shepherds of Christ – in black.

And then the hero of the piece, the Minister of Finance, who spoke English well.

An impressive image, as if coming out of a Bronzino painting, at ease, slightly ironic about the topic:

'Italy's current problem is not the Catholic Church...' The buildings illuminated in the night looked beautiful. I should ring the ABC and tell them that the photographer was also very good...a lyrical line to the whole thing.

Marie, George and Blaise are visiting from Switzerland.

The little one has grown, four years old, excited, talking all the time in a language difficult to grasp, but which Marie understands very well – talk of pirates, boats, imaginary friends.

Marie had brought her notes on translation, and some of the translation in French of our trip to Tibooburra that will go into the magazine.

Sad reading now, Jurgis and Cameron Corner, and Michelle, the Aboriginal girl, who used to work with us, that we met on the way there...

Afternoon tea here.

R going further and further out. Silent.

As if the person who had lived inside had left. Did he recognise any of us? Difficult to tell.

He was waiting politely to be fed, to be given a drink. She, full of a motherly care bringing him things, and he – alone among strangers.

Sorting old letters came across Malcolm's letter from Melbourne. *The First Journey* had been published and he bought a copy.

Was writing enthusiastically:

'I came away from your book intoxicated by the sheer audacity of your imagery.'

Or: 'Above all, your writing demonstrates an abiding compassion for the experience of life and a belief in the essential dignity of the human being to surmount the indignities of the environment that at times seems completely indifferent and unyielding.'

I was reading it to Mother who was very impressed with it.

We talked of the book, of Pat Woolley, half of the publishing house of Wild and Woolley, who made the publication of the book possible, asking me for a manuscript, at a time when no one was asking me for anything.

Her energy, enthusiasm for the book, for books, her constant fight to see them published, advertised, bringing them to the attention of critics, the market, showing them at every opportunity – festivals, readings...

In a biography of Martin Sharp by Joyce Morgan. Remarks of his mother about his religious beliefs:

'There is only possums up there.'

The full moon perfectly round.

The moonlight on the white wall of the terrace, the shadows of the leaves of the lime tree, as mysterious as when I was a child.

May

Concert at the NSW Art Gallery – Slava Grigoryan and Sharon Draper, a marvellous cellist, very warm full tone, marvellous phrasing and an elegant presentation.

The program – Vivaldi, Granados, Schubert – the *Arpeggione Sonata*.

By comparison to the cello, the guitar, a rather small sound.

At night listening to a program marking the anniversary of Bruno Walter. A woman was talking about him, his musicianship, how he taught her to sing, phrasing, tone...

She was very enthusiastic, full of admiration, she finished by saying that Bruno Walter was always trying to reach THE SUBLIME.

Later discussing the notion of the sublime with Vivienne, and she:

'The sublime went out with Kant.'

Re-reading Virginia Woolf's *Mrs Dalloway*, her style as if an alive surface, as if a skin that feels every movement, a light touch that maintains your interest.

Septimus, the psychiatrist, Lady Bruton, a very bitter irony to both portraits, more than bitter, savage, and Miss Kilman, quite ferocious – I did not remember this aspect in her writing.

In a new biography of Eugene O'Neill, his view of marriage: '...you become a part of another person and it is frightening...You start trying to beat your way out...'

Looking at the latest *Companion to Australian Literature* – we appear in a subsection called ETHNIC MINORITY WRITING. After so many years of writing here we are still totally outside the whole scene. Not only Ethnic, but Minority as well – a double blow...

The literary scene, as the sports scene and so on, seems to be dominated by a few names, as if written by adolescents who can only remember one name, more names in a scene impossible to sustain...

Mary in New York in the hospital after the stroke...the phone engaged for a long time. Then Mary answered, speaking well, at ease and very sociable, but she did not know who I was.

I was explaining...my name...do you remember other friends? Vassy? Yes, of course she remembered Vassy, but I was no longer in the computer.

Chitchat about her rehabilitation, she does not read but watches television, the news mostly, and then she asks in this very polite, distancing voice:

'And who are you, my dear?' I said goodbye after that.

Abado conducting Mozart's Requiem in Salzburg with the Berlin Philharmonic in memory of Karajan.

Conducting without score, gathering them all, the large Swedish choir, the soloists, the orchestra, gathering them delicately, with soft, slow movements, singing the words at every entrance.

A young soprano with a beautiful voice, singing at the beginning of the piece, then disappearing...I was very moved by her voice...

June

Cartoon in the *Financial Times* by Clementi. Two men talking, one asks:

'Why would Neil Armstrong want to talk to accountants?'

And the other:

'One last opportunity to explore a barren, lifeless world.'

The current coach of the Socceroos, responding to a woman journalist with a quotation from St Paul, I think, that women should not speak in public.

All full of themselves, constantly trying to reinforce their superiority, like people uneasy with themselves.

To the Danks Street Gallery to see Marea Gazzard's exhibition.

Marea – simplicity, subtlety and something noble in her shapes. She looked thinner than before. I was telling her how uplifting it is to see her work.

In the gallery around her a group of women friends in wheelchairs.

Looking from the door, as we went out, it seemed as if the hand of time had passed over us all.

Tom Stoppard, an interview by Geoffrey T. Hellman, published in the *New Yorker* in May 1968.

Tom Stoppard was in New York to receive the Tony Award for his play *Rosencrantz and Guildenstern Are Dead*, as well as for the publication by Knopf of his novel *Lord Malquist and Mr Moon*.

'The action of the novel,' he said, 'takes place within twenty-four hours in contemporary London. The characters have a sort of eccentricity that moves them into a Surrealistic context, but the book isn't in the least Surrealistic.

'Nothing in it is unreal or distorted, although some of it is heightened to a degree of absurdity, I think that realism has room for absurdity.'

'Things you write tend to go off,' he said, 'like fruit. There are very few things I've written that haven't tended to decompose, later on, before my startled gaze – this is perfectly natural, since literary material isn't mineral but organic, and nature changes...'

July

Prokofiev and *The Love for Three Oranges* at the Opera House.

A fast, colourful, animated production. Very good ensemble, designs and costumes, as if a Russian production of the thirties, full of imaginative details.

The opera written in the twenties when he was in America – a very young composer. We are behind the times here. They should produce *The Fiery Angel*, that would be something.

Vivienne last night:

'I am deteriorating.' Her assessment. I laughed.

'We all are.'

This is it, in a nutshell.

To Canberra. Driving into the landscape, the presence of people that have gone, have left us.

At the Paragon Cafe, a full house for lunch.

They were eating fish and chips, T-bone steak, and drinking milkshakes.

Historic food.

'Sarah'
I shall fall asleep, she said,
in spite of our anxious voices
plans for a possible cure.
I shall fall asleep
and she did, for the last time,
in a small hospital room,
to emerge in a blue box
her name on the cover,
next to his, her old passport
with the photo of the young
vivacious, elegant woman
placed on the small table
at the golf club.
Elderly friends listening
to the story of her life,
which they knew already,
then travel to the edge
of the golf course
a view of the sea, far away.

We bowed ceremoniously
as the ashes were scattered
over the small trees

in the valley below
as the rain began to fall,
softly.

August

Another program on the Greeks, the Trojan War, western ideas about the Greeks, little comes out of it except the realisation that all these western transformations of the Greeks are somehow artificial.

What remains is an instinctive people trying to deal with all this darkness, fear, forces out of control inside and out, and a constant desire to reach out, to rise, to capture in some distilled form the essence of things.

We go on watching Thebes, Oedipus's palace, the walls, the jewellery, sackings, destruction, imperialism, Mycenae, the house of Atreus...

What has remained, it seems to me, are stories of excessive brutalities and then the compassion for life, and the reinforcement of a moral law that does not let such things go unpunished.

In the *TLS* an article by Michael Greenberg, who is reading the letters of Thomas Berger, the American novelist...

'...it is 1974, Berger is working on *Sneaky People*...the progress of which his publishers insist on monitoring as he goes along.

'They want to guide him on how to begin his book – in a way that will enthral the reader immediately.'

Berger refuses to cooperate.

'My way of writing is the only one available to me.'

He explains glumly, and the publishers withdraw a portion of his advance.

At the Brisbane Festival, a long time ago, the organisers distant, no time to speak, preoccupied with some other administrative details.

Very lonely. Empty streets in mid-afternoon heat, modern buildings, glass, anonymity.

Crossing the mud-coloured river to the Cultural Centre, the same feeling of desertion, a few elderly people on benches, or young people in front of the gallery.

Only Thea Astley, crossing the road towards me, smoking her cigarette, and greeting me as if an old friend.

The session that I remember now was her session in which she was quoting Stow's poem – 'The Land's Meaning' – and Mudrooroo's.

He looked better than when I saw him in Lincoln, thinner now, older, read well this marvellous, very funny, bitter satire about Captain Cook and Alan Bond.

Marvellous transpositions of the whole group of crooks, they were attacked by Peter Pan in Aboriginal mode, flying through the air to secret mountain tops, talking around the fire – cutting off Bondy's hand, so that he is paralysed and can't write cheques any longer...and so on...very bitterly funny.

Marie Rambert talking about Nijinsky:

'I use the word "genius" advisedly. I am sometimes asked what

I mean by this highly evocative but imprecise word.

'In answer I can only say this:

'The dancer Nijinsky was once asked how he managed to leap so high. He is reported to have answered that he saw no great problem in this. Most people, when they leapt in the air come down at once.

'"Why should you come down immediately? Stay in the air a little before you return, why not?" he is reported to have said.

'One of the criteria of a genius, it seems to me, is the power to do something perfectly simple and visible, which ordinary people can not, and know that they can not do, nor do they know how it is done, or why they can not begin to do it.'

September

Thinking of friends that have gone, and the new poem by Merwin, 'Telephone Ringing in the Labyrinth', dedicated to Adrienne Rich:

'It is you, it can only
be you calling and I cannot answer'

The surface of life like a lake, we fall in, we disappear.
The surface closes with no trace.

Looking at papers I found Margaret Whitlam's obituary. She and Gough met during the war when he was serving in the RAAF.

He proposed:

'We might as well get hitched, don't you think?'

She said of him in 2002:

'I am a bit tired of the adulation. He's almost reached the

beatification stage. I suppose canonisation will come with the obituaries.'

The weather marvellous, warm, a slight breeze, a very blue sky... People described as – A YOUTUBE SENSATION.

To the Paddington RSL with Anna and Hilik to hear Monsieur Camembert and his band playing Klezmer music.

We came early to have dinner, the large restaurant full of elderly people, as if an unknown army, formed by social forces we were not familiar with.

As we left the table, they all turned, white haired, with the movement of sunflowers following the sun. They too were looking at us as if we were a totally unfamiliar type of people.

Prizes were being called out, and on the rack, these large parcels of meat waited.

We went upstairs to hear the band, very good, amplified, a stirring rhythm, the musicians all wearing these de rigueur hats of Eastern European musicians, a violin, a double bass, sax, trumpet and guitars, and a vocalist singing:

'My heart belongs to Vlady...'

Watching the flower pots through the kitchen window, I thought of Father, standing in the same spot, looking at the grey light and telling me:

'As if I am at the edge of an abyss, ready to fall in.'

I trying to divert him, and he:

'What do you think death is?'

Our relationships are changing now that we are using emails. Voices...essential things.

Voices, constantly resonating in my head, bringing their personalities – James with his impeccable pronunciation, Kate – strong, interesting sounds...

October

Speaking with Yolanta about our travels and how sad that we are no longer going anywhere. I talking again about our trip to Willandra Park...

...We arrived at the park mid-afternoon. The place totally deserted. A note on the notice board from the ranger that we were to go to the Men's Headquarters. No one there either. We went out to explore the place.

A golden light was falling on things. Past a small bridge we entered a large enclosure. At the back, a wall of trees, green and dense. A path between the two lawns and all around roly-polies arranged symmetrically as if in a formally designed French garden.

Silence. Near the trees, a large group of kangaroos, families with large males, females and children, all watching us, with interest. Mother and child coming closer to watch us, but still keeping their distance, standing on their tails, scratching their armpits as if disinterested onlookers.

But the place had an eerie feeling about it as if of an unseen presence that seemed to pervade the golden light, so that I was suddenly afraid.

We spoke to the kangaroos, but as we approached to take a photo, from the back, the voice of a male warned them to move away, called them back.

The unseen presence was so strong that I was sure something would be visible in the photographs.

But there was nothing when printed, a rather dark place.

Thinking of travelling in the outback.

The mysterious presence of the earth, the animals, this constant giving – plants, trees, fruit...

The vastness, the light, nightfall, the moon in the dark sky, the stars, the brilliant star below the moon like a swallow of light.

Last night – moon eclipse, not seen from here, the sky covered in clouds, but the photo of the moon from other places, like an immense, heavy ball hanging in the darkness, a reddish colour.

These miracles everywhere that we take for granted.

Paul Valéry about Degas when old:

'Nothing could be more mournful than the disintegration of so noble a being in old age.'

November

A review of Plutarch's *The Age of Caesar: Five Roman Lives*. He wrote a lot, a lot has been lost. A late antiquity list specifies 227 titles, biographies, miscellaneous essays...The one I would like to get hold of is: 'On Praising Oneself Inoffensively.'

When one listens to R, his lovely surprise of an analytical mind at work. A few of them around and seldom in this environment.

An alive, intellectual movement, well caught, speaking from already what seems a long line of work analysing literature, looking at texts, applying a criterion of evaluation to them. A pleasure to listen to him.

Isaac Babel:

'A well thought out story doesn't need to resemble real life. Life itself tries with all its might to resemble a well-crafted story.'

Suddenly, seeing again the statue of the Surveyor-General in Wynyard Park, I felt closer to understanding why people have always carved statues – the reassurance of a human body in the middle of the trees, the ability to bring to life, in some direct, physical, palpable means someone that has died.

Jolanta and Jurgis reading a book by a Lithuanian academic in America, who has lived outside the country for many years, discussing Lithuanian traditions, myths, etc. as well as LITHUANIAN SOUP – apparently made with the head of a pig and the bottom of a rooster.

The pig signifying the earth, the rooster – fire...

We laughed in the kitchen. I said:

'No wonder you are slightly extravagant, eating such soups.'

A documentary on Celibidache, the Romanian conductor. His first visit to Romania after the fall of Communism. Rehearsals in the Ateneu, the great concert hall of Bucharest.

I went there with H to hear a concert. I must have been fourteen.

Celibidache was berating the musicians for allowing a man with no knowledge of music to be in charge of the music field. The locals were looking at him surprised. As if they had any say in the appointments.

Lots of rehearsals, then a marvellous old film when young, conducting the Berlin Philharmonic, an approach to music full of finesse, total involvement, understanding, a lived thing.

How impossible it is to define music, sounds that remain sounds or become music. Out of one hundred concerts three or four maybe in which music comes alive in a real way, a phenomenon that can not be predicted, but comes out of a group effort.

I liked him, he was speaking out of an essential approach, working at it, relative, the instruments must sing, close to the human voice.

The black-and-white film about him, brought back impressions of Romania, memories of a Swedish film, *The Phantom Cart*, with Mother and Father, at Passalacqua, the big theatre where films were shown.

The only thing I remember about it, was the skeleton driving the cart over cobblestones, the terrifying noise, and I going under my seat, so frightened, the sinister light, people's legs and Mother's hand stroking my hair trying to reassure me. I must have been five or six.

December

On the radio, the *Requiem* by Berlioz, sombre, reflective, beautiful orchestral score.

What harmonies, what utilisation of male and female voices, the orchestra – like a deep, continuous voice full of passion.

In his memoirs, Berlioz tells us the entire saga of the *Requiem* – *La Grande Messe des Morts* – written in 1837, when he was thirty-seven, I think.

The *Requiem* was commissioned by Adrien de Gasparin, the Minister of the Interior at the time. Berlioz describes him:

'He belongs to that small minority of French politicians who are interested in music, and to the still more select company who have a feeling for it.'

Originally, the *Requiem* was to commemorate the dead of the 1830 Revolution.

The Ministry would pay him a commission of 3,000 franks for writing it and would cover the cost of the performance at the Chapel des Invalides.

Then they changed their minds, they cancelled it, de Gasparin was retiring from the Ministry, then they came back, decided to commemorate the recent death of General Damremont and the French soldiers that had perished at the siege of Constantine, an Algerian town captured in 1837...

A massive composition, large orchestra, four brass bands, choruses and so on.

Berlioz: 'A success was absolutely vital for me, a mediocre result would be fatal; by the same token, a failure would destroy me utterly.'

But the work was a great success, after that Berlioz was running for many months to get the money to pay the musicians, the chorus, the soloists...months and months of it.

As regards his commission, they forgot all about it, nothing happened for months afterwards, and they only paid when he threatened to go to the press and provoke a scandal.

He finishes by telling us:

'...some opposition newspapers represented me as a favourite of the regime, a sort of silkworm feeding on the revenue, and flatly stated that I had been paid 37,000 franks for the *Requiem*.

'They merely added a nought to the sum which I had received. That is how history is written.'

Very sad news – Judith has died.

How did it happen?

She was visiting a few months ago, she looked well, spoke of her plans for the future, and some weeks ago she sent me her new book of poems – FEATHER BOY –

Thinking of her, that marvellous early poem comes to mind that seems to encapsulate her personality, her energy.

'Eskimo Occasion'
I am in my Eskimo-hunting-song mood.
Aha!
The lawn is tundra   the car will not start
the sunlight is an avalanche   we are avalanche-struck at
  our breakfast
struck with sunlight through glass   me and my
  spoonfed daughters
out of this world in our kitchen.

I will sing the song of my daughter-hunting,
Oho!
The waves lay down   the ice grew strong
I sang the song   of dark water under ice
the song of winter fishing   the magic for seal rising
among the ancestor masks.

I waited by the water to dream new spirits,
Hoo!
the water spoke   the ice shouted
the sea opened   the sun made young shadows
they breathed my breathing   I took them from deep water
I brought them fur-warmed home.

I am dancing the years of the two great hunts,
Ya-hay!
It was I who waited   cold in the wind-break
I stamp like the bear   I call like the wind of the thaw
I leap like the sea spring-running.   My sunstruck daughters
   splutter
and chuckle and bang their spoons:

Mummy is singing at breakfast and dancing!
So big!

Judith Rodriguez

Acknowledgements

Billy Marshall Stoneking's 'One Last Poem' was published in the journal *Transnational Literature* in 2015, and in *The Best Australian Poems 2016*, edited by Sarah Holland-Batt and published by Black Inc.

Mark Strand's 'Black Sea' was published in his book *Man and Camel* (2006) as well as in his *Collected Poems* (2014), both published by Knopf.

Copyright in 'Eskimo Occasion' by Judith Rodriguez remains with the poet's estate and is reproduced with permission.

Every effort has been made to trace copyright holders and to obtain their permission for the use of copyright material. The publisher would be grateful if notified of any corrections that should be incorporated in future reprints or editions of this book.

About the author

Antigone Kefala has published three works of fiction, *The First Journey*, *The Island* and *Alexia*, and five poetry collections, *The Alien, Thirsty Weather, European Notebook, Absence: New and Selected Poems*, and *Fragments*, which won the 2017 Judith Wright Calanthe Award and was shortlisted for the Prime Minister's Literary Award for Poetry. There are three collections of journals, *Summer Visit*, *Sydney Journals* and this final work, *Late Journals*, all published by Giramondo.